USING CHILDREN'S BOOKS IN PRESCHOOL SETTINGS

A How-To-Do-It Manual

STEVEN HERB AND SARA WILLOUGHBY-HERB

HOW-TO-DO-IT MANUALS FOR SCHOOL AND PUBLIC LIBRARIANS

Number 14

NEAL-SCHUMAN PUBLISHERS, INC.
New York, London

Published by Neal-Schuman Publishers, Inc.
100 Varick Street
New York, NY 10013

Printed and bound in the United States of America

Library of Congress Cataloging-in-Publication Data

Herb , Steven .
    Using children's books in preschool settings : a how-to-do-it
manual for school and public libraries / Steven Herb and Sara Willoughby-Herb.
        p.   cm.
    Includes bibliographical references and index.
    ISBN 1-55570-156-6 :
    1. Reading (Preschool) -- Handbooks , manuals , etc.   2. Children-
-Books and reading -- Handbooks , manuals , etc., I. Willoughby-Herb,
Sara.   II. Title.
LB1140.5.r4H45   1994   94-8238
372 . 4--dc20   CIP

To Annie, Maggie & Sylvie

Thanks for allowing us to share children's books
long past our own childhoods.

CONTENTS

ACKNOWLEDGMENTS

Thanks to all the children who have brightened our professional lives through their unbridled joy in the presence of children's books. It is from those children that we continue to draw our ideas and motivation. We wish to acknowledge the children and parents of Shippensburg Head Start, the toddlers and parents who have attended Shippensburg Public Library's toddler times over the years, the Shippensburg University students who have conducted the sessions, and the hundreds of parents and children who have participated in the preschool programs of the Dauphin County Library System these last 10 years with special thanks to the talented children's librarians who planned and successfully delivered those wonderful programs. Thanks especially to Lynn Cockett, Barbara Glenn, Vicki Laudenslager, Valerie Moore, and Carolyn Patt. And, to the children and parents of the Rowland School for Young Children's nursery classes, thanks most of all.

We wish to offer thanks to all our colleagues who have shared their enthusiasm and ideas for using children's books through the years. We especially acknowledge the contributions of Lisa Murphy and Barbara Marinak, the President and Past-President of the Children's Literature Council of Pennsylvania; Barb Bartels, the School Librarian of the Rowland School at Shippensburg University of Pennsylvania; and Betty Arnold and Lisa Moyer, the Supervisor and Administrative Assistant of the Education Library, The Pennsylvania State University. We also acknowledge with gratitude the expertise of Peggy Myers and Nancy Struble in the preparation of this manuscript and offer special thanks to Jamie Myers for his technical assistance. Very special thanks go to Abigail Newberger, Shippensburg Head Start's Education Coordinator and to Charlotte Klein, Rowland School's First Grade Teacher for their creative ideas. And to Virginia Mathews, our editor and friend, we owe more than can be listed here, but we selectively acknowledge her sound advice, nearly endless patience, and continuing inspiration to all who work with children and books throughout the land.

INTRODUCTION

This book has grown from numerous talks, workshops and lectures we have presented about using children's books with preschoolers, to child care personnel, nursery school teachers, Head Start teachers, public and school librarians, kindergarten and prekindergarten teachers, reading specialists, special educators, administrators, parents, and university students. The advice presented is based on activities conducted with preschool children. The books recommended have been shared with preschool children and their parents and caregivers.

The overarching theme for *Using Children's Books in Preschool Settings* combines three major elements. The first theme states that children's books are crucial in the lives of children. It is a rare child who becomes a good reader without exposure to children's literature in the preschool years. It is perhaps even more unusual to find a reader who loves to read who didn't first love being read to in the preschool years. Literacy is the foundation upon which most childhood and adult learning is based. One only needs to examine the illiteracy rates in prisons and juvenile detention centers to know where a lack of learning opportunity can lead. Children's books are the steel, flint, and tinder for a lifetime fire of passion for the printed word. We simply need adults to open the pages and share those words and pictures to ignite the sparks. Our children's futures depend on adults who work in preschool settings. Those jobs are not always valued by our culture nor are they going to make anyone wealthy financially, but they are among the most important jobs in our country for the profound effect they have on children. And children's books are the single most powerful tool available to ensure that the profound effect one has on children is a positive one.

The second theme for *Using Children's Books in Preschool Settings* is our use of child development information to guide our choices of children's literature and the activities and strategies for using that literature. Chapter 1 contains the most direct evidence of that theme in its discussion of the link between children's literature and child development. Chapter 1 provides the rationale for this link and can serve as a reference source for the librarian or teacher who will organize a workshop or training package around the topics presented in the book. Especially helpful for that purpose, or for anyone who wishes to link children's development to children's book activities, will be the lists provided at the conclusion of Chapter 1. Children's Developing Abilities are presented for five age ranges (birth through six months, six to 12 months, 12 to 18 months, 18 to 36 months, 36 to 60 months) as well as Adult's Supportive Techniques for those abilities, within each age range. We trust this guide will prove helpful in the selection and use of children's literature for all children from birth through age five. Chapter 2 also focuses on the child development theme by providing strategies to enhance the most crucial link between the child and the book—the development of language. Communication strategies that facilitate adult/child conversation and creating environments that support oral language are the two approaches taken in Chapter 2 to forge the language link between child and adult, and ultimately, between child and book.

The third underlying theme for the book rests in the belief that people learn by doing. Though the format of a book means that people must read to receive the information presented, we have made the information as accessible as possible so the readers can use that information in their own settings. We have organized chapters around types of children's literature. For example, general types of literature are covered in Chapter 3, while a specific look at poetry and song and its importance in preschool settings is covered in Chapter 7. We organized chapters around strategies for using children's literature—planning storytimes in Chapter 5; reading aloud and storytelling in Chapter 6. We organized chapters around strategies for making the environment of the preschool setting conducive to the use of children's literature—setting up the storybook corner in Chapter 4; integrating literature experiences into children's everyday activities in Chapter 8. In all these chapters, information is organized and presented in list form wherever possible, with specific children's books and resources named by title. Additional titles are presented in the appendixes so that the reader can select a useful strategy and find many books that would serve that strategy well. Chapter 5, (Planning for Storytimes) contains actual storytime plans and starter plans for toddlers and older preschoolers in addition to helpful hints for planning storytimes. Chapter 9 (Connecting with Families to Support Literacy in the Home) acknowledges the importance of the home environment in the lives of preschool children and provides specific strategies for involving parents, with a special look at fathers in preschool literacy efforts.

Our emphasis throughout the book is the hands-on use of children's books with all children. We have suggested strategies for working with children who may have learning difficulties. We have also taken care to list books which portray children from all the cultures and in all the situations represented in the United States, but our first priority was selecting excellent children's literature. Any given children's book cannot be the answer to every question, nor can each book portray every child or be suitable for all children. A story serves best when told well. Illustrations inspire most when they combine with words and deliver a package such that one cannot imagine the story without the illustrations nor the pictures without the words. By selecting a broad and diverse collection of excellent children's literature, developing strategies for using that literature with all preschool children, and actually using children's books, everyday with every child, we can help children love books and fully appreciate the extended benefits of lifelong literacy.

1 CHILDREN'S LITERATURE AND CHILDREN'S DEVELOPMENT

Hey, my kitten, my kitten,
And hey my kitten, my deary!
Such a sweet pet as this
Was neither far nor neary.

Here we go up, up, up,
Here we go down, down, downy;
Here we go backwards and forwards,
And here we go round, round, roundy.

(from Marguerite de Angeli's
Book of Nursery & Mother Goose Rhymes)

INTRODUCTION

Good children's literature is truly a developmental gift for the child who comes to know it. Consider how the rhyme above provides a perfect early learning scenario. Picture a caregiver with baby snuggled to shoulder, walking and gently bouncing to the word patterns in this rhyme, moving the baby up, down, backwards, forwards, and roundabout while chanting the words. Imagine a loving, social exchange between baby and caregiver: the baby who enjoys being held, listening to the rhyme, predicting and feeling the motions that accompany the words, and the caregiver who with love and satisfaction learns to weave the rhyme and its accompanying actions into one of baby's daily routines (walking about the house, picking baby up after bathing or diapering). This and many of the nursery rhymes and songs we have used for hundreds of years while entertaining and soothing babies, are fine examples of the kinds of lessons that help babies learn language during their first years of life. The amazing endurance of these rhymes is a testament to the wisdom of their authors' intuitions about raising babies who are happy, sociable, and ready to learn their native language.

As we shall see throughout this book, a close relationship exists between good children's literature and effective learning experiences for young children. Strong as this connection is, however, another ingredient is needed to make the relationship most beneficial for children—a caring and knowledgeable adult. This adult (who might be a parent, caregiver, librarian, or educator) can be thought of as a mediator. In this case, a mediator who knows a great deal about children and about children's literature; and who can use this knowledge to create enjoyable and meaningful literacy experiences for children. This adult is able to use the right expressions and actions to keep an eighteen-month-old listening to an entire poem, choose stories that will delight a group of three-yearolds, or ask questions that will help a four-year-old understand a complicated story. When children have the good fortune to live with, be cared for, or taught by adults with this kind of skill, their language development is given quite a boost. Moreover, when children's family environments provide little if any of this kind of interaction, it is essential that we professionals are conscientious in providing these children with nurturing literacy experiences.

We believe that the ability to provide nurturing literacy experiences must be rooted in an understanding of children; and so we begin this book with a look at how children typically grow and develop. Although our focus will be on the development of literacy skills (speaking, listening, reading, writing), we may at times discuss other developmental areas (e.g., motor or social development). Most learning is inter-connected in the early years. Throughout the book we will refer to the principles and information contained in this chapter as guidelines for choosing and using literature with young children. We hope you will return to this information as you read the following chapters, and as you plan your own literacy programs.

THE DEVELOPMENTAL POINT OF VIEW

The study of child development tells us

1. how children's abilities grow and progress over time, and
2. how we can nourish and encourage that development.

For those interested in promoting children's literacy, an understanding of child development helps when choosing the kinds of literacy experiences that fit children at particular developmental periods, and helps to design successful ways to interact while these literacy experiences are shared with them. Today's early childhood and language educators (Bredekamp, 1987; Teale & Sulzby, 1989) value Lev Vygotsky's and Jerome Bruner's theoretical ideas about learning. The developmental principles and research in the following sections are based on their extensive work.

HOW CHILDREN'S LANGUAGE ABILITIES PROGRESS

Russian psychologist Lev Vygotsky (Wood, 1988, pp. 24-25) studied early social interactions between young children and their caregivers. He believed that the *content* of that interaction was of critical importance, specifically, that it should match the child's growing abilities. Think about the parent and child playing with the rhyme, "Hey, my kitten," as described earlier. Consider how that play matches the kinds of learning that typically occurs when an infant is between four and eight months of age. For example, during this developmental period, babies busily learn more and more balancing skills as they get ready to crawl, stand, and walk. So when the caregiver lifts or pulls the baby up, down, and around, to the rhythm of the words, the baby busily adjusts her balance and vision to each new perspective. Babies of this age are also learning to connect the words they hear to the objects and actions they see. The baby who is fortunate enough to have a caregiver who enjoys playfully repeating this rhyme, will soon anticipate being lifted when the adult pauses and says, "up, up, up," etc. Indeed, the content of this play does match the baby's increasing abilities.

In order to assist us in matching the literacy experiences we plan to children's growing abilities, we have prepared lists which summarize language development across the preschool years. Turn now to those lists at the end of this chapter (The Growth of Language Skills from Birth to Five Years) and notice that the left column identifies important abilities that children are developing during each time period. When we read these lists, we see that particular kinds of literacy experiences fit each developmental period. For example, in the case of sharing a book, we would adapt to children's development in these ways:

- For a three-month-old, choose a book whose illustrations contain large faces. Watch the baby's eyes gaze at the pictures, and name what baby sees.
- For a six-month-old, choose a simple concept book. Point to items in pictures and name them for baby. Encourage baby to point to familiar pictures.
- For a twelve-month-old child, choose a simple story that portrays familiar events such as going for a walk, eating, bathing, and going to bed. Encourage the child to help you turn pages, to imitate some familiar words in the story.
- For a two-year-old, choose a simple rhyming storybook. Encourage the child to join in after repeated readings. Sometimes ask the child to name objects in the pictures, or to tell you what a character is doing.
- For a four-year-old, choose a storybook with a simple storyline. Work on reading the story through to the end. Help the child understand any difficult concepts by relating them to her experiences. Encourage the child to retell parts of the story.

We can also use these developmental sequences to help us understand how children typically learn language so that we can provide environments to support children's own efforts to learn. When you read the developmental progressions through five years of age, you will notice some consistencies in how language develops:

1. Children learn to understand language before they actually speak. For example, at 18 months, a child can point to her body parts when requested, but will not necessarily be able to name them herself. This developmental principle (listening before speaking) reminds us that we should talk to children so that they will learn to talk, sing to children so they will learn to sing, and read to children so that they will learn to read.
2. Children play at language before using it purposefully. Playing with language characterizes *each* developmental time period. For example, a three-month-old plays at making sounds while babbling, but a four-year-old plays at reading by retelling memorized parts of storybooks and plays at conversations by talking to herself. Children learn language by playfully "trying-out" new sounds and expressions, by making mistakes and sometimes even correcting mistakes on their own. Clearly, we support language development by providing opportunities for language play.

3. Children use language imitatively before they use it for communication. Again, at each developmental period, we see children learning about language through imitating others. Opportunities for young children to imitate words, intonations, and body language as well as listening to others talk, help them become good conversationalists themselves.
4. Children's first language is concrete and based on their experiences (e.g., they say names of family members, request food). Abstract words such as "big" or "cold" are used in the later preschool period, and only after many concrete experiences (carrying big blocks, eating cold ice cream) with those words. We help children understand language by providing them with concrete experiences.
5. In the case of language, it seems that "practice makes perfect." We see young children practicing when they babble, play pretend, retell stories, recite songs and rhymes, and repeatedly ask questions.

In summary, we use information regarding children's developing language abilities in two ways. It helps us choose experiences that fit children's development and it helps us identify and provide for the basic processes (e.g., imitation, playfulness) through which children learn language.

HOW ADULTS SUPPORT CHILDREN'S LANGUAGE DEVELOPMENT

As we have just seen, one way to encourage language development is to be certain that children have opportunities to practice their own developing abilities. This provides that match between the child's ability and the content shared by the adult interacting with the child that Vygotsky recommended. Jerome Bruner (1960), extended Vygotsky's ideas by exploring the give-and-take that occurs during those interactions. According to Bruner, true learning requires not just a match, but a genuine involvement and mutual interest in one another. Adults who are genuinely caring and interested are more likely to remember what makes a young infant laugh, to reread the book with baby's favorite pictures, and to know what baby means by "goo-gotz." The sensitivity that develops from a nurturing relationship with children makes that adult an ideal partner in language-learning. Children's literature is a perfect vehicle for creating the occasion and substance for that learning. Sharing stories and rhymes with children easily invites interaction with the adult reader: questioning and answering, predicting what will happen next, laughing at shared humor, snuggling together for the scary parts. Literacy experiences provide perfect situations for genuine and mutual involvement. Researchers investigating Bruner's ideas (Garton & Pratt, 1989, p. 33-60) conclude that young children learn better when nurturing adults give them certain kinds of assistance. Those of us who work with children should try to use the following techniques during our daily interactions with children:

1. Make your language interactions interesting to children in earliest infancy by using a style uniquely suited to young listeners. This style, often called "motherese," involves making good eye contact, using simple and short statements, with soft but exaggerated intonations.

2. Allow many opportunities for turn-taking. Even the earliest language involves both listening and then reacting. When a two-month-old baby takes turns babbling with his father, he is actually trying out the fundamentals of conversation. The father listens and looks at the baby while he babbles (speaks). When the baby stops, the father takes a turn at talking while the baby watches (listens to) him. The three-year-old who has just heard the story of the "Three Little Pigs" and exclaims that the wolf is "bad" shows us that she understands the story and wants to express how she feels. To maintain her language skills, she needs someone to read to her and to respond to her feelings about the wolf. This need to be thoughtfully spoken to, read to and responded to, is especially important since children learn to understand language before they learn to express themselves with speech. The three-year-old listener understands much more of the story of the "Three Little Pigs" than she is able to express, but with many opportunities to hear the story again, she will learn to retell much of it herself. Throughout life, in fact, language development is dependent on the availability of this basic turn-taking. We need people to give us input, to listen, to answer us, to communicate so that we in turn can internalize, process information, and reorder it to our purposes.

3. Provide opportunities for children to learn language while they are exploring and learning about the world around them. This makes the language learning more meaningful and memorable. For

example, use the words "warmer" and "cooler" while your child is playing with cooked playdough. Bake gingerbread cookies to accompany the reading of "The Gingerbread Man" if you want your young listeners to understand why those animals all said, "Stop, Gingerbread Man! I want to eat you!" Remember that even though preschoolers are developing many language skills, they still learn new concepts best through concrete, manipulative, and sensory experiences.

4. Encourage the child's competence as a communicator by:

- Responding to the child's signals. For example, look when your toddler says, "Oh, oh!" Walk over, smile, and talk with the baby about whatever prompted her "Oh, oh!" Likewise, listen and answer when the preschooler says (for the thirtieth time that day), "Do you know what?"
- Remembering and providing opportunities for the child to practice his new learning. For example, remember the page of the book in which three-year-old Billy found a "B like my name." When reading it again, remind him to look for the letter B. All learning takes practice, and the adult who remembers the particulars of a child's discoveries, can encourage the practice and true assimilation of that skill or understanding.
- Focusing more on the content of what the young child is communicating than on pronunciation, grammatical expressions, or spelling. Children will make errors as they learn to speak, read, and write. They will eventually correct themselves as they experience correct models, but we must not deter these early efforts by correcting errors too soon.
- Reinforcing children's new learning and attempts at new learning. We need to show children that we are pleased with their efforts and accomplishments. Let them overhear us talk about how amazed we were when they joined in on reciting a new rhyme. Let them discover their pictures posted on the bulletin board. Take a photograph of a child's first attempt at writing her name on the chalkboard.

5. Provide appropriate language models for children by:

- During interaction and conversation, using sentences slightly longer than the child's. For example when a two-year-old hits a picture of a dog in a book and says, "Bow-wow," the adult reader says, "Yes! The doggie goes, 'bow-wow.'"

- Expanding on a child's expression to make it more specific. For example, when a three-year-old says, "drink," the adult says, "Do you want to . . . drink *milk* or . . . drink *juice*?"
- Using pauses, phrasing, and emphasis deliberately so that children can more easily focus on the important words. We call this "marking" the words. In the previous example, the adult paused before specifying each type of drink, and also emphasized those words. Young children learn to pay attention to the message when we emphasize in this way.

6. Build opportunities for conversation, language play, singing, and reading aloud into your daily routines. Make certain that these times are ones in which the experience can be relaxed and social, times in which the adult is able to pay close attention to the child, to respect the child's initiative (e.g., to select the story), and to truly interact around the language experience.

PUTTING IT ALL TOGETHER

From the theories of Bruner and Vygotsky along with the research-based techniques of Garton and Pratt, derive what today's early childhood professionals consider to be the "best practices" for encouraging young children's language development. The tables on the following pages are presented to assist you in incorporating these practices into your work with young children and their families. For each of the five age ranges in the tables, you will find a list of language abilities that typically develop during that time and suggestions for ways adults should interact with children to support those newly developing abilities. These suggestions are merely specific examples of the "best practices" recommended by developmentalists. Readers with experience in caring for young children are likely to have additional ideas for activities they have discovered as well.

We recommend that you use the information included in these tables in your program planning by:

- Reading over the specific tables appropriate to the age group with which you are working.
- Being certain that the activities you plan allow children to practice some of the developing abilities listed for that age group.

- Using as many of the methods suggested under supportive techniques as possible.

When we use these guidelines for planning literacy experiences with children, we can be certain that our story hours, language circles, parent education programs—all our planned activities—are firmly grounded in knowledge of children's development.

THE GROWTH OF LANGUAGE SKILLS FROM BIRTH TO FIVE YEARS

In using these lists, we ask you to remember that language growth does not occur steadily. Sometimes children take large steps ahead, sometimes they regress to less mature levels. Development often goes back and forth before stabilizing at any one level for a period of time. It is also important to consider that there will be variation among children's patterns of progress. Language growth appears smooth and easy for some children, and is attained only with great effort by others. Given these restrictions, we hope you will find these tables useful. Throughout the rest of this book, we will continue to view and present children's early literacy experiences through these windows on child development.

Birth Through Six Months

Children's Developing Abilities	Adult's Supportive Techniques
recognizes, attends to familiar voices, sounds and words	smile and talk to baby during routines (feeding, dressing), remembering to pause to let baby take a turn
quiets when picked up	take baby on looking and listening tours, pointing out and naming interesting items
communicates varied emotions	imitate baby's vocalizations, taking turns, positioning your face 12-18 inches from baby's so you are easily seen
attracts and holds attention of caregivers through vocalization	always use language as well as affection when greeting baby
smiles when interacting with others	at meal or conversation times, position baby where she can watch as well as hear the flow of language.
interacts with varied family members	sing songs, recite poems while rocking, riding, etc.
takes turns in gazing, smiling, pretend conversation with another	use language in a predictable manner, e.g., when finishing diapering always say, "All done!" When baby hits water in tub, say, "Splash!"
babbles with vowels mostly	expose baby to a variety of pleasant sounds—music, bells, music boxes, ticking, rattles
coos and babbles with expression and gesture	provide baby with toys that make varied sounds, toys that are interesting to explore
repeats pleasurable activities	"read" simple books to baby, by pointing and naming or using short, expressive sentences. Choose a few books that baby likes, and reread them regularly
enjoys investigating surroundings	include sturdy board books among baby's playthings
seeks out and holds small objects	note the times and places where baby enjoys playing with sounds—allow baby plenty of time to do this
tries to imitate adults	notice the sights, sounds, actions that interest baby; and label them—"doorbell," "doggie," etc.; after a time use the word just *before* baby will see or hear it
recognizes pictures of human face	when talking to baby, use short phrases, expression, interesting intonation.
	respond to baby's attempts to get your attention—allow baby's attempts at language to capture your interest
	respond to and guess at baby's attempts to communicate, e.g., when baby laughs at jack-in-the-box, mother says, "You like that don't you . . . Again?"
	when baby begins to babble, note which sounds ("goo-ga") she enjoys, so that you can use these to initiate her babbling

*Please note that in the case of prematurity, we expect children to behave according to norms adjusted for their prematurity (we subtract the number of weeks or months of prematurity), not according to expectations for a full-term baby. In most cases, premature children do catch up, but their developmental lag is more noticeable during the first two years of life.

Six to Twelve Months

Children's Developing Abilities	Adult's Supportive Techniques
takes turns in, initiates, and responds during verbal-motor play—such as Pat-A-Cake, waving bye-bye	continue using clear, simple language when talking to baby
babbling includes consonant sounds (b, m, g, etc.)	recite rhythmic poems while bouncing baby on knee, e.g., "Trit-trot to Boston"
understands simple, frequently used words such as no-no, give, eat	pay attention to and reward baby's attempts to verbalize
vocalizes during play	integrate language into baby's play times, not just naming objects, but using verbs and modifiers, too. For example, "Teddy *fell down*." "Teddy is soft."
vocalizing includes some regularly repeated syllables, e.g., "dee, dee, dee"	show baby some hand and finger rhymes, e.g., "This Little Piggy" and "Two Little Blackbirds"
tries to imitate adult speech	try to get baby to imitate words related to the sounds she babbles, e.g., if she makes "ba-ba-ba," encourage her to say, "ball" while playing with it
by 12 months, uses one or two meaningful words	continue turn-taking and pretend conversations
understands most simple language directed toward her	experiment with baby's following easy directions: "give Mommy a kiss," "kick the ball"
puts objects in and out of containers	read simple concept book to baby, point to and label something on each page; after repeated readings encourage baby to point to a particular item (choose something she has been interested in)
uses thumb/finger grasp	
pokes/points with index finger	make sure that cardboard books are among the playthings baby can carry about; if baby brings book to you say, "Shall I read?"; go ahead and read it
creeps or crawls	place books on furniture edges so that baby will discover them while "cruising"
pulls to stand and cruises	routinely use clear, predictable expressions when interacting with baby, e.g., "All done!," "Bye-bye," "Again?"

Twelve to Eighteen Months

Children's Developing Abilities	Adult's Supportive Techniques
enjoys watching and listening to others speak	encourage dramatic play by acting out situations with child, e.g., pretend to go grocery shopping
babbling includes intonations and some real words	continue to join child in play, but be certain she has times to play alone as well
uses more than 3 words; 20-50 words by 18 months	provide large paper, crayons, paint brushes, chalk, finger paint, playdough, for developing eye-hand coordination
begins using simple sentences	continue to reinforce child's attempts to imitate and use language; when child tries out new words, repeat the words enthusiastically after her, showing your understanding and pleasure with her efforts
points out pictured objects, family members in photos	
still uses gestures along with talk to communicate wants	
begins pretend play with familiar roles, e.g., "cooks" with pots, "feeds" doll or self with empty spoon	when possible follow child's ideas in games and play, but balance turn-taking
begins to use sentences, but still uses one word to communicate a longer message, e.g., "cookie" means "Get me a cookie."	continue to expand upon child's utterances, modeling simple, complete sentences, for example when child drops a cookie and says, "Oh dear," say "Oh dear, the cookie fell down!"
enjoys playing alone at times; has favorite toys	choose storybooks with simple language child understands, and books with rhymes and songs
imitates caregivers, using gestures, words, intonations, expression	choose toys child can use for imaginative play, dolls, cars, animals, kitchen items
walks, balances and carries objects	make sure child has durable books so that she can "read" and turn pages independently
uses language to get adults to pay attention	
enjoys books as toys, and as a way to interact with others	when reading to child, ask her to find familiar items in pictures
turns pages of sturdy book	
uses crayons with supervision	make sure that storybook reading is part of daily routine
uses action words, e.g., go, drink	
understands simple directions by 18 months, e.g., "Put the book on the shelf."	set aside a shelf or space that child can reach, so that she can find her own books and put them away

Eighteen to Thirty-six Months

Children's Developing Abilities	Adult's Supportive Techniques
begins to understand simple prepositions, e.g., in, out, up, down	continue holding conversations with child, behaving as if she can understand and contribute competently, even if you have to fill in a bit for her now and then
answers questions with action words, e.g., will tell that the baby is "crying"	teach children new words daily by talking about what you are doing, what is happening, e.g., "Daddy has to write Grandma a letter." "We must find yogurt at the grocery store." "Mommy is fixing the broken chair."
points to body parts when requested	
enjoys listening to and sometimes joins in on songs, rhymes and stories	accept your child's speech, rather than correcting her mistakes
begins to understand abstract words, such as big and little, my turn	spend at least 15 minutes reading aloud each day
understands 2,000-3,000 words by 36 months	begin to use the public library regularly, taking child along if possible
uses many two-word sentences (duos), (e.g., "more milk," "doggie allgone") by 24 months; uses 3-5 word sentences by 36 months	sprinkle the environment with good reading material; books in the car, every room
has a vocabulary of 50-250 words by 24 months; 500-1,000 words by 36 months	introduce child to "real" stories—short ones with bold illustrations, simple folktales (The Three Bears), cumulative tales (Gingerbread Man)
names pictured objects	
tells whole name	ask child about pictures in book while reading, "What's Goldilocks doing now?"
begins to use pronouns, modifiers, plurals, past tense; uses I or me when referring to self by 30 months	provide child with small toys (e.g. toy people and house) for imaginative play; use directional (up, down) words, and prepositions (inside, on) while playing together
speaks clearly most of the time, yet still uses language playfully sometimes making up words	provide child with toys for creative dramatics, e.g., puppets, dress-ups; and for constructing models (e.g., building blocks, snap blocks)
asks questions	
begins to recite songs and rhymes independently	provide child with materials for "writing and drawing"
imitates vertical strokes of crayon	continue enjoying songs and rhymes, especially ones that can be acted out (e.g., Where is Thumbkin? Jack Be Nimble)
enjoys side-by-side play with peers	take cues from child about how she likes to be read to (Some like to be curled up in your lap; others like to be building with blocks four feet away! What matters is that they enjoy hearing the story.)

Thirty-six to Sixty Months

Children's Developing Abilities	Adult's Supportive Techniques
understands most adult language	try to read stories through to the end, asking questions as as you go to keep child's interest
enjoys hearing stories, has some favorites and by about four years knows parts of some "by heart"	as you read, make sure child can see pictures and talk about them before turning the page
answers simple questions	encourage child to join in as you read familiar or repeated phrases
uses longer sentences (4 + words) and words	
talks to self during play	occasionally point to a word, or move your finger from left to right under the print as you read
vocabulary continues to grow so that by 5 years has a 3,000 word oral vocabulary	ask child to "read" or tell you about a favorite book
uses more grammatically complex sentences, e.g., uses varied verb tenses, uses connecting words such as—but, and then, actually	encourage child to read public print when you are out together
still invents some words, e.g., refers to clothing being "inside out" or "outside in"	post signs that the child can read, e.g., names of helpers for the day, the word "snack" on snack tin
pronounces most sounds correctly by 60 months	make homemade books together, using photographs, pictures cut from magazines
understands some concepts of color, shape, numbers by four years	reread books as often as requested; probably child is trying to memorize them
during the fifth year, counts to three, draws a person with three parts, attempts to write name and to copy a circle and a cross	provide opportunities to follow verbal directions
retells stories, recalling wording from the book	encourage child to try simple writing tasks, x's or signing name to letters, making M on a paper to remind family to buy milk
begins to recognize/"read" some public print, e.g., sign for favorite fast food store, label on box of cereal	keep drawing and writing materials available
begins to recognize concepts about print, such as— beginning and end of books, the fact that there is just one right way to read the words in a story, knows to separate words when writing	encourage child to act out stories, constructing props such as stick house for the "Three Pigs"
by age five—	use words and phrases from stories read, e.g., "run, run, as fast as you can!" from the "Gingerbread Man"
*dictates "stories" for adults to write,	when getting library books, sample from the wide array available: fiction, non-fiction, poetry, etc.
*tells simple jokes,	when writing yourself, talk about what you are doing and why, e.g., "This card will really cheer up Uncle Paul."
*asks HOW and WHY?	
*converses with peers,	when printing for child, use large clear letters; and sometimes talk about them, e.g., "Letter i is a straight line with a dot on top," "T makes the sound t-t-t-t"
*follows a sequence of three instructions,	
*learns songs and rhymes through imitation	continue to be deliberate in the language you use with children, so that you are providing opportunities for the child to learn new words

RESOURCES ON DEVELOPMENTAL PROGRESSIONS AND SUPPORTIVE TECHNIQUES

Kaye, K. 1982. *The mental and social life of babies: How parents create persons.* Chicago: University of Chicago Press.

Morrow, L. M. 1993. *Literacy development in the early years: Helping children read and write.* Boston: Allyn and Bacon.

Pflaum, S. W. 1986. *The development of language and literacy in young children.* Columbus, OH: Charles E. Merrill.

Powell, M. L. 1981. *Assessment and management of developmental changes and problems in children.* St. Louis, MO: Mosby.

Willoughby-Herb, S. & Neisworth, J. 1983. *HICOMP preschool curriculum.* San Antonio, TX: Psychological Corporation.

BIBLIOGRAPHY

Book of Nursery & Mother Goose Rhymes by Marguerite de Angeli. Garden City, New York: Doubleday, 1953, p. 89.

REFERENCES

Bredekamp, S. (Ed.). 1987. *Developmentally appropriate practice in early childhood programs serving children from birth through age 8.* Washington, DC: National Association for the Education of Young Children.

Bruner, J. S. 1960. *The Process of Education.* Cambridge, MA: Harvard University Press.

Garton, A. & Pratt, C. 1989. *Learning to be literate: The developent of spoken and written language.* New York: Basil Blackwell.

Teale, W. H. & Sulzby, E. 1989. "Emergent Literacy: New Perspectives" in *Emerging literacy: Young children learn to read and write*. Strickland, D. & Morrow, L. (Eds.). Newark, DE: International Reading Association.

Wood, D. 1988. *How children think and learn*. Oxford, UK: Basil Blackwell.

2 CHILDREN'S ORAL LANGUAGE DEVELOPMENT

Speaking and listening abilities play a central role in preschool children's learning, in both cognitive and social-emotional development. Likewise, learning to speak, to listen and to converse are tasks that go hand-in-hand with a young child's first book experiences. In their discussion of how to create ideal environments for literacy learning in the early years, Neuman & Roskos (1993, p. 89) state that "much of the benefit of storybook reading resides in the collaborative talk that actually surrounds the book reading event." We find that adults who are already skilled in talking with children will most likely be successful in sharing literature with children. They are able to help direct the child's attention to important parts of the story, to relate the story to the child's own experiences, to assist the child in understanding key words and story elements, to help the child become involved in the story's actions, and to encourage the child to explore ideas in the story. The sharing of a storybook becomes a natural extension of already occurring, comfortable language exchanges in which both parties take turns in telling, asking, and answering.

In the last chapter we reviewed several ways in which adults can help young children acquire language (speaking, listening, reading, writing) skills. You may have noticed that most of these involve language exchanges or "conversations" with the child. Those of us who work regularly with young children are aware that it is not a simple matter to engage preschoolers in conversations, especially when you are not a family member. Certainly, good preschool classrooms are noisy places, full of language, but as we look from child to child, we can always find some who talk very little or not at all. For these children, in particular, it is important that we are knowledgeable and deliberate in our efforts to encourage their developing oral language abilities. But adults must realize that all preschool children are almost always more comfortable in using language in their own homes and with family members and others they know well. Helping these children feel safe and comfortable in expressing themselves in the nursery school, child care center, or library are major goals for those of us who work with preschoolers. Furthermore, because the exchange of conversation between a child and a more mature speaker (teacher, librarian, parent) is so firmly at the base of learning language, we should regularly encourage all preschool children to talk, to listen, to converse, and to use their developing language abilities for learning.

In this chapter we will consider two approaches to encouraging children's oral and conversational language: *communication strategies that facilitate adult/child conversation, and creating an environment that supports children's oral language.* We will end the chapter with a consideration of language learning for children with special needs.

ADULT/CHILD COMMUNICATION STRATEGIES

ADULT ATTITUDES TOWARDS CHILDREN'S LANGUAGE

Research has demonstrated that by talking to, responding to and interpreting young children's early speech in particular ways, adults can help children learn language better (Bruner, 1980; Kaye, 1982). This involves the adults' attitudes as well as their behaviors. In fact, the attitudes that adults express toward children's early language are just as important as any techniques they use to help children learn to talk.

What are the important attitudes shown by effective adults? They pay attention to children while talking to them, and are able to adjust their own styles of communication (adding emphasis, expression, re-wording) to help children maintain interest and understanding. They carry on their conversations at the child's eye level, further indicating their commitment to understanding one another. They talk about concepts that are important to children and that help children focus on and maintain interest in their activities. When they are listening to a child and attempting to interpret what the child is saying, they show caring attentiveness and often credit the child with greater understanding or ability than is readily observable in the child's speech. For example, when the child says, "Ball all gone," the adult might assume that the child is both commenting that the ball is missing and asking for help in finding it. The adult assumes that the child means to communicate more than the words alone say. Finally, these adults regularly make efforts to engage children in conversation, giving them opportunities to take a turn, and rewarding even minimal participation with attention, enthusiasm, and praise. The regular attention of interested, child-focused adults seems to help children feel comfortable in expressing themselves orally as well as trying their best to communicate with others. The presence of adults who use this nurturing conversational style, results in greater language learning in preschool children.

In addition to adopting this nurturing style, there are specific techniques that adults can incorporate into their interactions with children that will assist in children's language learning. These are techniques that will help adults in getting conversations started with children. We will explore six here: *Self Talk, Parallel Talk, Leading Statements, Affirming Responses, Modeling Varied Uses of Language,* and *Questioning.* In general, these techniques will be described beginning with those which are least intrusive for the child. Therefore, it is good to begin by using self talk with children who are least comfortable in conversing with adults. Note that we listed questioning last, since questioning is one of the most difficult ways to encourage young children's use of language. In fact, direct questioning can be so threatening to children that it sometimes results in their being non-verbal and shying away from the questioner. This is especially true of children with language delays.

SELF TALK

This involves the adult playing near the child and talking in descriptive ways about what she (the adult) is doing. For example in putting together a puzzle, the adult says, "I'm looking for the corner pieces," "Now I'm looking for a piece of grass to fit in here." Or, when building with blocks, the adult says, "I hope I can stack all the red ones before my building falls down."

This kind of language often draws a child's attention to the adult's play, and in turn, to the adult's purposes. Often the child shows his understanding of and interest in the adult's goals by helping to find the particular puzzle piece or helping to find all the red blocks. Without speaking, the child has safely joined in on the adult's conversation, because the child chose to join and would be free to leave the interchange when desired. There was no question to answer correctly or incorrectly and no requirement for language, and finally, non-verbal communication was perfectly adequate. The wise adult will respond kindly to this mode of conversation from a child, allowing other opportunities for interacting, but not requesting any greater participation until the child initiates it.

Even children who do not interact as a result of the adult's self talk, are likely to watch and listen, learning some words and expressions that will be useful to them in their own playful explorations. For example an observing child might learn how the concepts of corner pieces and color-matching are useful in putting together jigsaw puzzles. The adult's self talk is a form of "thinking aloud" and thereby provides children with a model for using language and labeling to help solve problems. Sometimes the adult's "thinking aloud" proves so interesting to a child that he will imitate the play and talking. For example, while drawing a simple picture the adult says, "My person will have red hair, and I'm going to put a hat on him." The child drawing nearby may say, "My person will have brown hair, and I'm going to put a hat on, too."

In summary, a child's response to the adult's self talk might take a variety of forms, from merely watching and listening, to imitating, from participating non-verbally (finding the puzzle piece mentioned), to joining in on a verbal exchange ("Look, I found another red one!"). At each level, however, we see that the child is involved in some turn-taking conversation with the adult.

PARALLEL TALK

Much like self talk, this technique doesn't require any speaking at all from the child. We merely use words that, in this case, accompany the child's activities as we watch her playing or exploring her surroundings. For young infants this may be in the form of our saying the names of objects, events, and people as the baby looks at them. This parallels the infant's learning to recognize objects. We provide the appropriate verbal label for the objects the infant is interested in. With a toddler, we would use simple sentences which describe the objects that the child is playing with ("You picked up the yellow car."), and describe actions the child is engaging in ("You're making a tower."). When children are three, four, and five we can provide parallel talk that describes many of the subtleties of their activities. For example we can describe how a building the child is making is changing ("The base of your house is getting longer."). We can describe how objects have multiple characteristics ("That is a lacy, pointed snowflake you are cutting."). It helps children learn words when we attach them to their play in this way. By providing the words that stand for real objects and experiences we are helping build a bridge between their concrete world and their mental world.

Certainly parallel talk builds a child's oral language vocabulary. The child hears, remembers, and may repeat specific words used by the carefully speaking adult. In addition, children often become motivated to interact and converse with the adult who is using parallel talk. Sometimes they show their interest in what we are saying by deliberately changing their play, to hear what we will say about that! They are taking a turn in the conversation in a non-verbal way, as they offer a new activity and watch and listen for the next parallel talk statement. We often see children smile, acknowledging their hypothesis about what we would say. Children also converse with the parallel talker by playing in a way that acknowledges their understanding of what they have heard. For example, Alec, a five-year-old boy with a severe oral language disorder, was sorting through a container of colored blocks. His teacher, using parallel talk, pointed and said, "You have a red block in this hand and a blue block in this hand." Alec responded by finding all the blue blocks and piling them on his left, and piling all the red ones to his right. Though he never said a word, his actions said a great deal. He heard what his teacher said, he can differentiate red from blue, and that color idea led to a good play routine. The teacher continued to describe these actions, taking her next turn in the conversation.

As with self talk, parallel talk may lead into an actual verbal exchange or conversation with a child, but this is not a necessary outcome. The child is participating in the conversation through his continued activity, which then gives the speaking adult more to describe.

LEADING STATEMENTS

Certain expressions ("I wonder . . . , I hope . . . , I think . . . , I'm afraid . . . ") when properly drawn out, invite children's completion of the statement. The important characteristic of these leading statements is that they are merely "invitations" not "requests" for verbalizing. Consider the following examples. While reading a version of *The Gingerbread Man,* the adult turns the page then looks at the picture before reading and says, "Now, I wonder who's going to be chasing him?" The child points to the pig and says "piggy." The adult's statement didn't necessitate, but merely invited a response. While playing in the kitchen area of the preschool, the teacher pretends to cook some vegetable soup, serves it to some children at the table and says, "I hope it tastes . . . good?" One child says that it is "good" even before the teacher finishes the statement. In still another example, story hour is over, and the librarian looks and points out the darkening sky saying, "I bet it's going to. . . . " A child finishes her statement with, "Rain!" Had a child not finished either of these last two leading statements, however, the adult could easily have completed them, and no child would have felt a need to speak at that time. It is because such statements do not pressure children, though, they often do inspire children to join in the conversation.

AFFIRMING RESPONSES

This technique is used when the child has begun speaking to the adult. The adult's first important role is to regularly answer or respond to the child, showing the child that what she says is important. Secondly, the adult's response should show both an interest and an understanding of what it was that the child said. For example, when a child points to a picture and says, "piggy," the adult affirms what the child said by saying, "Yes, I think the piggy will chase the Gingerbread Man!" Repeating something of what the child has said, always lets the child know that she was heard. Of course, the child easily recognizes enthusiasm in the adult's response. After we adults communicate to children that we heard them, and that we accept what they said, we will at times want to expand on what they said, in order to help build their language skills. In the example above, the adult added the content about the pig chasing the Gingerbread Man, thereby demonstrating the addition of a verb and the use of a whole sentence.

In early childhood education, we do our best teaching by starting at the child's level, regardless of the content. So certainly in the language area, our best language lessons begin with a statement already made by the child. As we affirm the child's statement we can extend it, add a leading statement, or even follow up with a question. At these times our personal knowledge of the child becomes important, so that we can "remember for" the child who is building a store of words, concepts, and expressions. For example, while the librarian was reading *Rosie's Walk,* four-year-old Chuckie continued to say, "Sadie." The librarian who knew about his pet said, "Chuckie, I believe this story reminds you of your pet chicken, Sadie." Chuckie smiled broadly then asked to take the book home after story hour. Had Chuckie instead been told to be quiet until the story was over, he would have been discouraged from associating his personal experience with the story in the book. We find that most young children do not interrupt us unless they have something important to say. Yes, they will eventually have to learn not to interrupt, but now, just when language is blooming and preschoolers are trying to use it for thinking and communicating, we should be as affirming as possible in our responses to what children say.

MODELING VARIED USES OF LANGUAGE

As we converse with and speak to young children, we need to remember that we are continually providing models for their speech. In addition to acquiring new vocabulary, they learn a great deal from our language: how to take turns in conversation, how to be polite listeners, how to greet others, how to make people laugh, how to assert one's rights, and so on. Michael Halliday (1975) theorized that language develops in young children according to its usefulness in their everyday life. Children develop intentions or purposes long before they have the words to express themselves. As they become mature language users they develop vocabularies and language styles to fit these varied purposes. Unfortunately, some children are exposed to very limited language use in their homes. For some children most language they hear is directed toward satisfying one's own needs ("I want my dinner now"), or controlling language ("Pick that up. Stop that!"). Those of us who work with children ought to be conscientious about modeling language across its varied uses. According to Halliday, young children should be learning how to use language to interact socially, tell about themselves, learn, imagine, and communicate information to others. Fortunately, these functions of language are clearly related to children's enjoyment of literature. For example, we can engage children in conversations about books by encouraging imaginative language. While reading *A Snowy Day* by Ezra Jack Keats, the teacher says, "Let's pretend this is a snowy day, and we have to get bundled up to go outside." The teacher's language tells the child that we can think about the "there and then" as well as the "here and now." When we talk about how a story book character feels about something that happened, we are showing the child an example of how language helps us communicate socially. When we ask the child's opinion about a turn of events, we are encouraging the child to use language to tell about himself. When we review what happened before continuing on in the story, we use language for learning. When we retell a story, we use language to communicate.

It is crucial for the child who seldom hears or participates in good conversation at home to be exposed to children's literature. Showing children there is something else in the world beyond their home, beyond their center, can sometimes open a child up to a lifetime of ideas and dreams. And even if children's books only provide entertainment or a brief distraction in the here and now, that still represents an excellent use of a child's time.

QUESTIONING

Finally, we focus on how to ask children questions, remembering that this is the most fragile of all the conversation starting techniques. Questions are not necessary for making conversation with children. Children respond quite readily to the techniques already discussed. Preschoolers themselves seem more comfortable using statements as conversation starters, saying to someone who is playing with a dog, "I have a dog." So we should use questions with children when we sincerely want to know something, e.g., "Can you remember who drew this picture?" We use questions when we want to encourage the child's thinking.

Pitfalls to Avoid

Because some questions can easily shut down children's conversations, we begin with some cautions, some don'ts, about questioning. First, don't let your questions intrude upon the child. We should respect children's privacy as much as we would an adult's. For example, don't ask them personal questions about their families, what they ate for breakfast, do they like their sister, etc. We must also be careful that our questions do not invade the child's activities. We are struck by how often a well-meaning adult comes upon a child busily engaged in an activity (such as drawing) and, disregarding the child's activity, asks a totally unrelated question, "Did you go visiting over Thanksgiving?" It requires quite a lot of self-control for a child to stop drawing, stop thinking about the drawing, recall the holiday activities, and politely answer. In fact we need to remember that during the preschool years it is still very difficult for some children to talk at all when they are involved in a project. Even talking about the project itself can be distracting to them. A second caution is not to overdo the questioning. Again, well-meaning adults often ask question after question in an effort to maintain conversation with the child. If you find yourself doing this, and the child is giving short, polite replies, move on to one of the conversation techniques discussed earlier. You can be fairly certain that these kinds of replies indicate that the child is merely trying to satisfy the questioner, rather than being inspired to extend his thinking or to contribute something to the conversation. The child is likely to view the verbal exchange as more of a pretend conversation or even a "test" than a true conversation in which ideas are shared.

Respect Children's Answers

From these two cautions, we proceed to some guidelines for asking questions. The most important of these is to be prepared to listen carefully, accept, and respect children's responses. Adults need to understand that there are many possible reasons for children not being able to answer questions. Sometimes the child may know the answer but not be able to find the words needed to express it. Often when we ask children to tell us about their drawings, they know what it is they are making (e.g., the buds on a tree) but they don't know what the object or part of the object is called. At other times children just don't know how to phrase the answer.

When we ask children questions, we need to be prepared to pay careful attention to their answers so that we can help them communicate what it is they really want to tell us. Sometimes children's answers remind us that they don't always interpret words as we do, they sometimes understand language in very literal ways. Many of the "cute" stories we tell about preschoolers involve the differences in the way they interpret language—the child who responds to her mother's question, "Can you take the cupcake wrapper off yourself?" with "I'm not wearing a cupcake wrapper!" While these misunderstandings entertain us and provide us with treasured anecdotes, it is important that we not laugh at our children's efforts to communicate. Children overhearing adults laugh at what they say, or retelling their misunderstandings and miswordings, can become timid or embarrassed about speaking.

Finally, respecting children's responses means respecting their periodic wishes not to be questioned. Preschool children are known for their candor, and will typically let the questioner know their lack of interest—often they turn or walk away. Consider that questioning as a technique for encouraging children's thinking is not common to all cultures, so we should not assume that all children are equally comfortable with it.

Ask Understandable Questions

Certainly the content of the questions we ask is related to their success in inspiring children's conversations. We do best by talking about the present (words like yesterday, tomorrow, and next month are quite confusing for preschoolers), about activities the children are currently engaged in and excited about, and about topics they have already introduced themselves. We also do best when we word our questions simply, using expressions the child has already used. For example, young Kenny tells us that he is going to wear a "Spook-em" suit for Halloween. Rather than asking if he is going to be a ghost, we could say, "Can you tell me about your Spook-em suit?"

Three Kinds of Thought Provoking Questions

Finally, we consider the kinds of questions that encourage children's thinking. When properly used, and not overused, this kind of questioning leads children to reason independently, thus seeing themselves as good thinkers and problem solvers. We will discuss three types of thinking questions: *Recall, Deductive Thinking,* and *Divergent Thinking.* Each of these three types of questions involves children in an important kind of thinking.

Recall questions involve simple memory, for example, "What is the name of your school?" or "What color is this?" When we ask children recall questions, they typically give us short answers. They either do or don't know the answer and usually don't spend a long time thinking about it.

Recall questions provide children with limited conversational experiences. Some can even be answered by a simple "yes" or "no." Unfortunately they are the kind that most adults ask young children: "What did you get for your birthday?" "Did you lose a tooth?" "How old is your baby brother?" On the other hand, deductive and divergent thinking questions are more complex. More mental or physical activity is needed in order to come up with a suitable answer. They lead into conversation more easily.

Deductive thinking questions involve the children in coming up with a correct conclusion to the problem posed by the questioner. For example, when we ask, "How many different animals chased the Gingerbread Man?", the child has to remember or turn back the pages to identify and count each animal in order to get the correct answer. Another deductive thinking question is, "Why did the fox want the Gingerbread Man to sit on his head?" The child has to remember the fox's state of hunger along with the cookie man's closeness to the fox's mouth in order to answer this correctly. The important characteristic of the deductive thinking question is that it *does* have one or more correct answers.

While deductive thinking questions can provide difficult challenges to children, we can help reluctant children attempt to answer these by including some leading statements within our questions. For example, "Can you find the word on the cover that says, "Gingerbread?"It seems to me that it's a really long word at the top of the page." Or, "How many animals chased that Gingerbread Man; let's see, one . . . two. . . . " Often these leading statements show reluctant children how to get started in their thinking about the problem posed in the question. But remember, if this doesn't work, one can easily model the whole problem solving strategy for the child if necessary and the young child will not feel put on the spot.

A third type of question is the *divergent thinking* question, which encourages complex thinking but which has no one correct answer. Most answers that children give are acceptable. These questions are sometime called open-ended for this reason. Divergent thinking questions often ask children to make judgments ("Do you think the little old lady should bake another Gingerbread Man?"); to make predictions ("What do you think will happen next?"); to imagine ("If you were the Gingerbread Man, how would you get away?"). Often the child's answer leads the questioner to ask more about the child's idea, to ask why or why not. Interesting, thoughtful conversations that involve sharing and acceptance of one another's ideas often follow divergent questions. These kinds of questions open children to a wider range of thinking, to more creative thinking, and to accepting other persons' ideas. Because of this, we ought to weave divergent thinking questions into discussions of books as often as possible.

ENVIRONMENTS SUPPORTIVE OF ORAL LANGUAGE

One of the most noticeable characteristics of the conversational language of preschool children is its changeability across various settings. Most children, for example, are much more talkative at home than at school or the library. However, there is much we can do to help children feel more comfortable about talking in situations away from their homes, such as preschools, child care centers, and libraries. We will discuss five techniques for planning environments that will encourage oral language.

PROVIDE CONCRETE, MANIPULATIVE MATERIALS

Children typically feel more comfortable in talking when they have materials to manipulate, as any of us who have ever conducted a "Show and Tell" will testify. Children seem open to talking about objects that are interesting to them, fun to play with, and that allow them to show as well as talk. Therefore we want to make sure that our classrooms and libraries have toys to play with, objects to manipulate. In the case of children's books, we can help children talk about the stories if we have some concrete materials available that are related to the stories. For example, if our spring storytime/preschool theme is Pets, in addition to book displays we can set up a table arrangement with interesting, related objects, both real and miniature. We could display items for pet care (leash, collar, brush, empty pet food containers), photos and pictures of pets, plastic animal models.

Because our programs often serve infants and toddlers as well as preschoolers, we may need to change some of our typical ways of decorating and arranging our spaces. Instead of relying on high bulletin boards with words and pictures to direct attention to monthly themes or seasonal changes, we need to use more three-dimensional displays. For example a table display for summer could simulate a beach setting by using a blue tablecloth with model fish, fishing boats, seashells, a bucket and shovel, sun screen, some books about the beach, and a large "Please Touch" sign. Consider using items that children can experiment with (magnets, lenses, nuts and bolts). These items hold children's attention and give them some meaningful experiences to talk about. Toddlers and preschoolers, alike, are much more inspired to talk about, wonder about, and develop enthusiasm for our theme than they would have had we merely made a beautiful poster.

In day care and preschool settings, it is good to gather collections of related books and toys. For example, during National Fire Prevention Month, when children visit the firehouse or host members of the fire department, arrange a play corner that contains miniature people, buildings, firetrucks, ladders, twine, and books about firehouses and firefighters. As we join children at play in this area, we can suggest through our own parallel play or through conversation, that the children act out some of the ideas in the books. This type of collection can be done with most themes we plan: Seasons, Animals, Plants. It can also be done across curricular areas. An arrangement of song books with musical instruments, dancing clothes and shoes, books about painting and drawing along with media displayed for children's use, or children's cook books along with various cooking utensils are all examples.

Another way of using manipulatives to encourage language is to make take-home projects that children will enjoy playing with (will even take out of their backpacks!) and that act as extensions of themes from school or story time. Make a dog puppet with the children after reading a story whose main character is a dog. Don't expect the children to enjoy playing with the puppet just because they made it, however. For many children, you will need to build the bridge to play. Encourage them to give their puppet-dog a name, talk about and show them ways to play imaginatively with the puppet (make it a bed, find it a toy to play with, use it to act out scenes from the story, repeat phrases and words from the story, use it to play a "trick" or joke on someone at home). This kind of take-home project might inspire language in several ways: prompting the child to strike up a conversation, to retell the story, to tell someone how they made the puppet, to enact scenes from the story using language from the book, or to make up new stories for the puppet. We will provide several other examples of take-home projects that stimulate language in later chapters.

Finally, preschool teachers and librarians might consider purchasing or making a second set of some of their storytelling kits (felt board sets, puppet sets) and displaying them on a "Please Touch" table next to the storybook so that children can use them to act out, retell, or remember the story.

PERSONALIZE THE ENVIRONMENT

Children feel more comfortable, and hence more talkative, in their own spaces. Help them feel some ownership of their schools and libraries, by regularly displaying their projects, by allowing them to assist in making the seasonal decorations, and by having their names incorporated in displays. Also, invite children to bring things in from their homes or neighborhoods for use in our programs. Ask children to pick up a pretty leaf or flower to add to a picture or bring a picture of food for making a nutritional display. Ask them to bring empty boxes to use for displaying collections. Of course, be careful to invite, not require, children to bring items to share. This kind of project usually involves parental cooperation, which is not available to all children. However, other children may enjoy bringing extras to share with a friend, and this results in an experience in thinking about and helping one another as well.

Another way we personalize environments for children is to make certain that they are knowledgeable about their surroundings. Teachers and librarians should consider how the space looks to a young child. What areas might catch the child's eye (story pit, table toys, book shelves, doll corner)? Which areas and items are important for the child to know about (bathroom, tissue and paper towel holders, check-out desk)? Then we need to give each of these a special verbal label, and be certain that the children know where the areas are and what they are called. We can do this by orienting children to the setting on their first days there, and by engaging them in activities that utilize their knowledge about this new environment. For example, in a preschool setting it would be fun for children to help make a book about their school building that contains pictures of significant people (principal, librarian, custodian, teachers) and places (library, playground, office). Children could take turns taking the book home to share with their families. In a library or preschool center, children would enjoy playing a game where they take a turn reaching into a surprise box, taking out a "long-lost" object, and returning it to its proper place.

INVEST IN DRAMATIC PLAY

The dramatic play center is an area that most inspires children to talk, narrate, and communicate. In a well-equipped and regularly changing dramatic play center, language, socialization, and problem-solving flourish. Change the materials in the dramatic play area often enough to keep up children's interest in playing and experimenting with roles. Add props that suggest settings to vary pretend play: kitchen, bakery, grocery store, doctor's office, restaurant, beauty shop, clothing store, gas station, school, newspaper office, bank, post office, theater, pet shop. Invest your time and attention in dramatic play as well. Children play longer and use more language during play when joined by an enthusiastic, thoughtful adult.

CONSIDER SOCIAL DIMENSIONS OF LANGUAGE

Some children are more comfortable talking with the teacher, or with just one peer, or chanting a rhyme with the whole group at circle time. Children benefit from one-to-one, small group, and large group adult-child communication. We should attempt to provide this range of experiences for all children, through our careful planning of the preschool classroom and the daily sequence of activities. For those children who have difficulty in expressing themselves, we should emphasize the type of situations that best evoke their language.

USE FACILITATIVE ROOM ARRANGEMENTS

Finally we need to consider how to arrange the whole environment/room in a way that encourages children's talking. Remembering that language emerges from play, we should consider what kind of language accompanies the play that goes on in each area of the room. Give consideration to children's need for quiet language areas as well as noisy areas. Children need quiet areas for listening to storybooks, for imaginative play with small toys such as doll houses, and for drawing and writing. The quietness in these areas will help children listen to adult talk directed toward them, help them feel that their statements and questions will be heard, contribute a feeling of privacy to their imaginative toy play. When we create a quietness in these areas, we actually stimulate language. On the other hand, children need areas where some noisiness is accepted—building with large blocks, driving ride-on vehicles, and group socio-dramatic play. Adults need to be certain that children have opportunities for both quiet and noisy language play, that one kind of play does not interfere with another. This is typically done by separating these areas in our centers, placing sound-absorbing materials in and between areas, and establishing guidelines for behaviors in each area.

SUMMARY

We began this chapter by discussing how important it is that children's first experiences with books involve conversations/communication around the book. From these conversations with adults, children learn much from storybook reading: learn the story itself, learn about life and people, places and objects, learn the meaning of new words and phrases, learn about print and written language, and expand their own ideas and possibilities. The effectiveness of these conversations, however, depends on our children being verbal and the adults who care for them being skilled in conversing with children. We described several techniques adults can use to initiate conversations with children as well as techniques that stimulate children to be more verbal. You may want to experiment with these techniques by trying out some of the following activities.

ACTIVITIES

1. Select a preschool toy (one with enough parts to share) and a partner who is willing to play the child's role. As your partner quietly plays with the toy, try out some self talk and parallel talk. Your partner may choose to join in the conversation by playing, talking, or both. Reverse roles.

2. Select and read a preschool picture book. Identify four different points in the story where you could use a leading statement to encourage a child's joining in on a conversation. Write down each leading statement, possible child responses, how you will finish the statement if the child doesn't.

3. Select and read a picture book, select a partner to role play the child listener. During the reading of the book ask three questions: a recall, a deductive thinking, and a divergent thinking question. Afterwards, ask your partner to evaluate your questions based on how genuine they seemed. Were they really relevant to that part of the story, or did they seem to be exercises in answering questions. Which ones inspired conversation best? If time permits, reverse roles.

4. Storybook reading often gives us an opportunity to expand on a child's vocabulary. We can teach precise names of objects by pointing them out in pictures as we read. Sometimes, however, we don't know the precise names of objects. We have to remember to expand our vocabularies as well. Peruse some popular picture books and locate objects for which you don't know the specific names (e.g., types of trucks, animals, plants). Find out the names and share your learning with a child the next time you read together.

QUESTIONS RELATED TO CHILDREN'S SPECIAL NEEDS

1. *What about children who have oral language ability, but select to be non-verbal in certain settings such as the library or preschool?*

Answer: Early childhood workers assert that this is a fairly common situation, so we must be prepared to communicate with these children. The key to our being effective is to establish and maintain communication with these children even though they don't respond verbally to us. We also do well to treat their quietness in a matter-of-fact way, rather than drawing attention to it. In fact parents often need to be reminded not to label children as "shy" or "backward," and to refrain from statements such as, "I don't know why she won't talk to anyone." Children who overhear such statements come to label themselves and to behave accordingly. Sometimes quiet children are actually very good listeners and thinkers, both of which are important aspects of becoming a good conversationalist.

We can help these children become more verbal by remembering that conversation grows out of functional communication between persons. So we work hard at showing these children that we care about their feelings, their needs, their individuality. We use parallel talk to describe their unique play activities. ("What a good idea to draw a book in her hand!") We acknowledge their facial expressions and other non-verbal communication. ("That was funny, wasn't it?") We allow them the opportunity to consider questions without having to answer them. ("I wonder how the fox will talk the Gingerbread Man into getting on his back?") We talk to them in all the natural, conversational ways described throughout this chapter, rather than ignoring them verbally. We make connections with the child, show him that he is important to us, and that the connection doesn't depend on his having to talk. Although we will be overjoyed when these children finally do begin talking, we should be careful not to react in a way that draws attention or makes the child feel that her non-verbal behavior has been a problem. By offering children our time and patience, by establishing a trusting connection in a safe, stress-free environment, we can encourage most quiet children to begin talking. If this interaction style is tried for several months without effect, of course, we should refer the child for intervention from an educational specialist.

2. *Aren't there some children who refuse to speak or avoid speaking for emotional reasons? If so, do we need to use different techniques in encouraging conversation with them?*

Answer: Yes, there are. We needn't use different techniques, but need to use them very sensitively and in a very customized manner.

A commonly occurring example of children whose emotional problems interfere with their language use are children who are abused. We will refer to these children in answering this question. Our answer is based on Patricia Crittenden's 1989 review of research on characteristics of maltreated preschoolers as well as how we can best teach them in preschool settings.

According to Crittenden, most preschool classrooms will have at least one maltreated (at least marginally maltreated) child, and special education classes are likely to have more. The results of these children's abuse can be seen in any of a variety of their behaviors: they may be compliant, passive, defiant, or generally disorganized.

Two important language characteristics of maltreated children are:

1. they avoid or are uneasy about interacting with other children and with their caregivers, and
2. when engaged in conversations with others they work hard to keep the conversations from being personal, detailed, or lengthy.

We can see that as these children have learned to cope with their abusive environments, they have also developed styles of interaction which make it difficult for them to participate in the many enriching experiences associated with good preschool literacy programs. For example, these children will not readily want to connect the events from a storybook to their own lives. They will not necessarily welcome an adult's use of parallel talk or even an adult joining their play.

The key to our success with these children will be our commitment to providing enriching language experiences for them, while being sensitive to the children's difficulty in participating in these experiences. That is, we must be patient and understanding, yet keep focused on the goal of sharing with them the joy and knowledge that come from literacy experiences. A very positive note that will motivate those of us who work with the youngest children, is the research finding regarding some abused infants' and toddlers' ability to change their behaviors according to whether they are in non-threatening or potentially dangerous situations (Crittenden & DiLalla, 1988). The researchers observed that some of these youngest maltreated children were able to behave with mere compliance when with their abusive parent, but could interact cooperatively when with nurturing adults. This reminds us of the many ways that good, early childhood programs can prevent future problems for the children we serve.

Crittenden suggests that adults who work with preschoolers who have been abused should provide three types of experiences for them:

1. create a predictable environment,
2. help them learn socially-appropriate ways to interact, and
3. teach them to communicate openly and trustingly.

Crittenden's three techniques fit easily into the models we have explored in this chapter. Let us look at them more specifically:

- Defiant children who are wary of our trying to coerce them into talking will feel much more comfortable with our use of self talk and even parallel talk than with questioning or attempts to force conversation.
- Passive and compliant children will appreciate our acknowledging the importance of any of their activities by describing those activities through parallel talk.
- Disorganized children can be helped to focus and extend their attention by the reinforcement that comes through our joining their play and modeling and describing play activities.

Crittenden's techniques can also be related to many of the suggestions for *Adult's Supportive Techniques* from the first chapter. In this case, we needn't only consider the suggestions for the child's actual age range, but rather look for suggestions for Supportive Techniques that would not threaten children, would not make them fret over being right or wrong, and would encourage their own first steps toward conversation. In fact, we may need to look for techniques suggested for younger children, since that child's language level may be less mature in certain ways. Suggestions from Chapter 1 follow:

- Noting the times and places where the child is most communicative and allowing plenty of opportunity for the child to do this.
- Respond as much as possible to the child's attempts to get your attention (when these attempts are appropriate behaviors of course, for example, looking your way, pulling on your arm).
- Use simple, clear language (especially when giving directions or asking questions) so that the child's language environment is predictable.
- Provide repeated experiences with language (that is, use poetry, song, predictable stories) when you wish to encourage the child to join in.
- When playing, follow the child's cues in language use and

imitate some of the child's play behaviors. Use words and expressions the child has used.

- Try to arrange opportunities for language turn-taking games such as peek-a-boo, animal noise games, and songs such as "Did You Ever See a Lassie?"
- Accept the child's speech and its content without correcting or criticizing.
- If possible, hold some "conversations" in which you behave as if the child is contributing even though you may have to fill in for her once in a while. For example, if the child is painting you might say, "I wonder what Amy is making?" When she allows you to look (by moving a bit), say "Thank you. I like this big, yellow sun you've made." "I wonder what you'll make now . . . (child says nothing, but continues to paint). . . Oh, yes, the clouds, of course."

3. *There is still another kind of child whose ranks are growing disastrously in our society: the child whose home environment provides neither the security nor the appropriate stimulation necessary for becoming a confident, self-assured learner. What special considerations should be made for these children?*

Answer: A child who learns to fear the world is apt to lose the natural proclivity for exploration, inquiry, or participation. A pervasive sense of danger or insecurity can cause a preschool child to "go into hiding" emotionally and psychologically. The strategies described in this book have increased significance for these children. Anything we can do, any hope we can deliver, any literacy skills we can foster, may help lead a child from that "hiding" place.

Pediatricians at the Boston City Hospital Pediatric Primary Care Center have found that a small act, the gift of a book to parents bringing their children for a visit to the clinic, has a strong effect on parent and child interactions at home. In the study, parents who received gift books were far more likely to make reading or book-sharing an important part of their preschool child's day. Significantly, the positive effects of the study were strongest for the poorest families (Needlman, Fried, Morley, Taylor, & Zuckerman, 1991). Young mothers, many of them unwed teenagers from the culture of poverty, need to be taught—and are often eager to learn—that talking, playing, and reading with their young children provides a bit of a shield and an antidote to their insecure surroundings. The work in Boston issues a challenge to librarians and teachers who work with preschool children and caregivers / parents, a challenge to work directly and also through other agencies, such as health clinics. Be sensitive to the circumstances of poverty. Have respect for the difficulties faced by the single mother, especially the teen mother, but also be unremitting in your day to day approach to using children's books and promoting that use among all parents. Remember that every book read, every story told, and every conversation held makes a difference in a child's life.

4. *How can we build conversation with children whose articulation problems make them difficult, if not impossible, to understand?*

Answer: This can be a frustrating situation. The difficulty lies in our learning to understand the children, since articulation training is rarely suggested as an appropriate language intervention for preschoolers. Many of us adults are no longer as flexible as children in understanding different dialects or speech styles.

As with selectively non-verbal children, we must first work on establishing a connection with the child. We should focus especially on the children's non-verbal communication abilities, use the parallel and self talk communication techniques when interacting with them. We maintain communication in ways that don't rely on the child's talking.

However, we do want to reward, encourage, and help develop the child's oral language; so we try to plan situations in which we can fine-tune our ears to what the child is saying so that we can become effective listeners and language partners for the child. This can often be done in parallel play situations with realistic toys (e.g., miniature farm, school, hospital sets, toy vehicles, dolls and housekeeping toys). Realistic toys are important because we can make pretty reliable guesses about what words the child is trying to say ("tractor," "ambulance"). We can also use parallel and self talk, and notice how the child repeats these words and phrases, thereby sensitizing our ears to the child's unique ways of articulation. We learn a lot about the child's language by reading together as well. Choose picture books with realistic pictures and pictures that parallel the story.

Spending a few minutes each day playing with the child in this way trains our adult ears so that we understand better and can become better conversationalists with the child. Try to save questioning until you have developed some skill in understanding a child's unique language style. Children do become frustrated when we can't understand their answers to our questions. Overall, though, in our experience these children already know that we won't be able to understand all that they say, but they appreciate our willingness to try and that we take time to communicate with them.

For children who have difficulty speaking because of a physical handicap such as cerebral palsy, it takes much time and effort for them to control their speech mechanisms well enough to be understood. We need to encourage their hard work by showing them our appreciation and attention, giving them time to form their words. We must also be understanding when their first easily recognized words are commands: "Stop," "No," "Mine!" These words are also popular in the toddlers' vocabularies. One of the first ways we use language is to gain control over the world around us, to assert our individuality.

Of course, some children may not ever be able to become effective verbal communicators and may need augmentative communication (pictures displayed on language boards, notebooks, or electronic assistance). When these children are included in our programs, it is paramount that we adults establish communication by learning to use the augmentative devices and that we encourage the other children to use them as well. Our efforts to do this provide us with a wonderful opportunity to teach children acceptance of individual differences in the true spirit of inclusion.

5. *Are special conversational techniques needed for children who are bilingual or non-English speaking?*

Answer: All the techniques suggested in this chapter are appropriate for these children. Basically, when children feel cared about and accepted, and are encouraged to converse and have appropriate language models, they will work at becoming fluent. If possible we should try to locate another teacher or volunteer who speaks the child's primary language. Arrange for that person to visit your setting. If this is not possible, consult with someone (parent, an ESL specialist) regarding the child's language use, so that you know about the child as a language user. When working with these children we certainly want to help them use the language of the school, but it is important to consider that young children learn language best when it is integrated into their activities, it involves their senses, and it involves activity. We can see that parallel talk, creative dramatics, exploring with objects, and personalizing the environment would all be fine facilitators for language learning.

For children who are truly bilingual, knowledge of a second language is very enriching. However, some children are forced to become bilingual before they have strong skills in their primary language. For these children we often see weakness in both languages, and the bilingualism is impoverishing rather than enriching. Although these children will learn English as they play with their peers, it is not adequate to rely on peer interaction for their language learning. When we observe children's language at play, we note that the language they use during child-child interactions is far less sophisticated (shorter sentences, less varied sentence structures, less specific vocabulary) than that which they use in talking with adults and in talking about storybooks. Therefore, conversations with adults and conversations about books are important sources of language development for bilingual children.

BIBLIOGRAPHY

The Gingerbread Man retold by Eric Kimmel. Illustrated by Megan Lloyd. New York: Holiday House, 1993.

Rosie's Walk written and illustrated by Pat Hutchins. New York: MacMillan, 1968.

The Snowy Day written and illustrated by Ezra Jack Keats. New York: Viking, 1962.

REFERENCES

Bruner, J. 1980. *Under five in Britain.* Ypsilanti, MI: High/Scope Press.

Crittenden, P. M. 1989. Teaching maltreated children in the preschool. *Topics in Early Childhood Special Education,* 9(2), p. 16-32.

Crittenden, P.M. & DiLalla, D.L. 1988. Compulsive compliance: The development of an inhibitory coping strategy in infancy. *Journal of Abnormal Child Psychology,* 16(5), p. 585-599.

Halliday, M. A. K. 1975. *Learning how to mean: Explorations in the development of language.* London: Edward Arnold.

Kaye, K. 1982. *The mental and social lives of babies: How parents create persons.* Chicago: University of Chicago Press.

Needlman, R.; Fried, L.E.; Morley, D.S.; Taylor, S. & Zuckerman, B. 1991. Clinic-based intervention to promote literacy: A pilot study. *American Journal of Diseases of Children.* 145(8), p. 881-884.

Neuman, S. B. & Roskos, K. 1993. *Language and literacy learning in the early years: An integrated approach.* Fort Worth, TX: Harcourt Brace Jovanovich.

3 TYPES OF CHILDREN'S LITERATURE

About a thousand children's books are published each year in the United States that might be considered appropriate for preschool audiences. Add to that a backlist of thousands of appropriate titles remaining in print one or two years after their publication (a few hundred many more years if they have attained the standing of "classics" or "standards"), and one has an idea of the difficulty a parent or caregiver, librarian or teacher faces in making the right choices of books for the individual child or group of children. In this chapter we will discuss the importance of children's literature and offer help in selecting books by discussing the important types of children's literature all preschoolers should have a chance to see, hear, and hold in their own hands.

THE IMPORTANCE OF CHILDREN'S LITERATURE

READING TO YOUNG CHILDREN HELPS DEVELOP THEIR LITERACY SKILLS

Researchers who study the development of literacy in young children, find that one of the most important experiences we can provide is to regularly read books to our children (Butler & Clay, 1985; Durkin, 1966; Taylor & Strickland, 1986; Teale, 1984). When we read daily to young children, we help them develop the following important literacy attitudes and skills:

- Most importantly, we teach them the joys of reading, motivating them to want to learn to read and to enjoy literature.
- We teach them important lessons about print long before they will learn to read. For example, children notice what some of the letters look like, notice that we move from left to right and top to bottom as we read.

- We talk with them about what we are reading and thereby teach them to understand "book language," which may be different from the spoken language that most young children hear.

Indeed, reading to children is the best way to prepare them to be readers. Reading also builds other language skills. Children who are read to a lot, are better conversationalists. They understand many more words because they have heard those words used in stories. When they speak, they borrow words and expressions from stories they have heard. Four- and five-year-olds who are beginning to write, often imitate wording from books. They try to spell "The End"—or they fill a paper with pretend writing that moves from left to right and top to bottom just like the words in books.

READING TO YOUNG CHILDREN HELPS THEM LEARN ABOUT THE WORLD BEYOND

Our experiences in reading to young children show us that the value of reading to children extends far beyond the development of literacy skills. When children, as preschoolers, learn to listen and understand stories, they learn much about their worlds, about themselves, and about others. When they become readers themselves, they can continue to enjoy these benefits on their own.

Children who are read to become much more knowledgeable about the world in which they live. Even as babies, they come to understand words such as animal names and colors. They understand concepts such as big, middle-sized, and small. As older preschoolers, book reading expands their understanding of the places outside their own world of family and community, their own place in time. They may learn names of dinosaurs, how to care for pets, or what zoo keepers do. And this kind of learning helps young children feel more comfortable as the world becomes more familiar; it also helps them feel good about themselves, to see themselves as competent learners.

Children also learn about themselves through being read to. As young toddlers, they learn that they like particular books, words, and phrases, or pictures in books. They love to find pictures of babies, especially babies who look like them. As older preschoolers, they relate their personal experiences to those of others through being read to. They come to understand their own environments of child care, of parents coming and going, of problems with sharing, when they are read stories that portray such events. Those who have learned to enjoy reading look to literature to help them understand themselves and their circumstances better.

In addition to self-understanding, children learn about others through books—to walk in someone else's shoes, to care about someone else, to be open to individual differences. With preschoolers, this often begins with animal stories, as they feel sad about a lost bear, or happy when a mother owl returns to her babies. Since many children's experiences are limited by their own community, we need to rely on books to teach children about people and places beyond their immediate lives. Good books that help children to care about and understand others are a fine preparation for living in a multicultural world.

Finally, as all of us who read to children know, when we have regular read-aloud sessions with children, we build a very special relationship with them. We have a storehouse of shared conversations as we have talked about stories. We understand one another's points of view as we have disagreed about what we think should happen in a story. We have common experiences in what made us laugh, what surprised us, what made us sad, because we know the same stories, and we have prepared ourselves for the future by talking together about serious events such as the death of a pet, or a parent losing a job. Reading to children is a delightful way to build the foundation of a long relationship. We come to know one another and our world better, humanizing both of us, children and adults.

SELECTING BOOKS

What a rich variety of books we find when we browse through books for preschoolers in libraries and book stores. There are board books, song and rhyme books, concept books, folktales, and many others. When selecting books for our early childhood programs, we should try to gather samples of all available varieties. In this way we are more certain of having books that will appeal to each child's individual interest. Furthermore, each type of book contributes something unique to a child's literacy foundation—the more types of books children are exposed to, the more they learn, recognize, and wonder about books. For each of the book categories that follow, we discuss their unique way of supporting children's literacy development, and we list some outstanding examples of books by noted authors and illustrators. We have not included poetry, nursery rhymes, and song books in these categories as they are the focus of Chapter Seven.

STURDY BOARD AND CLOTH BOOKS

Of course this type of book is the most often chosen for reading to babies and toddlers. These durable books can be washed and wiped, and withstand much handling by the infant just as soon as she is ready to pick up and carry objects. These books usually have few words, so they don't demand much listening from the infant. The finest of these have bold, bright pictures to appeal to the infant's developing visual abilities. In addition to infants, we also recommend these books for lending and home visiting programs where the books might be used by all ages of children in the home. And we recommend these books for preschoolers who are beginning to memorize books as a first step into reading. These books are easily memorized because the words are few, are printed clearly, and usually match the pictures. Preschoolers can be encouraged to read these books to their stuffed animals, dolls, and to their younger brothers and sisters.

Suggested Reading

Lucy Cousins. My Cloth Book series (Candlewick, 1992) includes these titles: *Flower in the Garden, Hen on the Farm, Kite in the Park,* and *Teddy in the House.* These are sturdier than most cloth books, and the illustrations are of bright objects outlined in black on colorful pages. They are perfect for babies looking at their first books, and for babies turning their first pages.

Amy MacDonald, author, and Maureen Roffey, illustrator. Their Let's Explore (Candlewick, 1992) series contains these titles: *Let's Make a Noise, Let's Do It, Let's Try,* and *Let's Play.* Toddlers will be attracted by the large pictures of other toddlers dressed in bright clothing. The culturally diverse characters ensure that most toddlers will find someone who looks like them in this series. Caregivers and parents will find some good suggestions within these short books for developmental activities to do with their toddlers.

Helen Oxenbury. Oxenbury's Baby Board Books (Simon & Schuster, 1981) and Big Board Books (Macmillan, 1987), remain favorites of young children and their caregivers. The simplicity of the illustrations in the Baby Board Books with their focus on the daily lives of babies, makes these very interesting "reads" for infants. The Big Board series is probably more appropriate for toddlers as the text and illustrations are a bit more complicated. The Big Board Books also depict children of varied ethnic backgrounds.

Sian Tucker. The chubby board book, *Colors* (Simon, 1992), will appeal to newly walking babies who enjoy carrying objects around. And what better object to carry than a book? The colors are printed in true tones and the color referred to in the text stands out clearly. This is a perfect first concept book as well.

FIRST STORYBOOKS

Most two-year-olds are ready to listen to and look at some simple storybooks. Look for books that tell short and clear stories with only a few words per page, with illustrations that closely follow the story. One of our goals is for children to learn to listen to and look at a whole book—story length is an important consideration here.

Suggested Reading

Margaret Wise Brown, author, and Clement Hurd, illustrator. *Goodnight Moon* (Harper, 1947). This classic has been a favorite first story for many, many children. It is now available in cardboard and pop-up versions as well. But it is the gentle rhyme and the bright pictures of the little rabbit getting ready for bed that capture young listeners. Many three- and four-year-olds have learned this story by heart.

Mirra Ginsburg, author, and Jose Aruego and Ariane Dewey, illustrators. *Where Does the Sun Go at Night?* (Greenwillow, 1981). This story consists of simple questions and answers, one per page. The questions are relevant to the experiences of very young children, such as "Who tucks him in?" and "Who is his Grandpa?" The illustrations are colorful, focused, and involve lots of animals.

Ann Jonas. *Now We Can Go* (Greenwillow, 1986). This book tells a simple story of a young child packing a bag for a trip. One by one, objects are taken from the blue toy box and placed in the red bag. The entire story line consists of twenty-two words, most of them referring to the pictured objects. The illustrations are bright and objects are easy to find. This is a great first story, and young children will enjoy pointing to the toys as the story is read.

Vera B. Williams. *"More, More, More" Said the Baby* (Greenwillow, 1990). This is a large, beautifully painted book, telling the stories of three toddlers and their interactions with their caregivers. Each of the stories can be read separately, or the whole book can be read at a sitting. The language used in the book is very realistic, with the caregivers using "motherese"—

"right in the middle, right in the middle, right in the middle of your fat little belly."

PICTURE STORYBOOKS FOR PRESCHOOLERS

These books, as with the previous category, contain stories and pictures that are closely related. In these books, however, the words and stories are a bit more complicated, the wording more like "book talk" than like the language that children use themselves. It is in stories such as these that children learn to understand wording such as "Once upon a time," or " . . . and then something surprising happened," or "When the day came. . . . " Therefore, these are books that children need to hear again and again in order to become familiar with the way that storybook language sounds.

Children learn to understand these stories through both pictures and words. In the finest picture storybooks, the pictures explain and add to the words. Both pictures and words are telling the story. Sometimes they take turns and sometimes they sing out together, but the picture storybook is a true collaboration of art and text. When we read these books to children, we want to give them ample time to look at the pictures so that they can enjoy and become skilled in figuring out the visual aspects of the stories as well.

Suggested Reading

Ezra Jack Keats. *The Snowy Day* (Viking, 1962). This story of a young African-American boy playing in the snow is a favorite of preschoolers. Keat's portrayal of the day's events in colorful collage pictures and a simple, sequential story line, will help children understand that their daily lives can also be stories to tell.

Pam Conrad, author, and Richard Egielski, illustrator. *The Tub People* (Harper, 1989). This book tells the story of an event in the lives of a little toy family, in which the tub child gets stuck in the bathtub drain. Don't worry, though, there is a happy ending and an assurance that this will never happen again. Preschoolers who like to act out stories with their play people, love the play ideas in this book. They are comforted by stories in which children who encounter difficulties are always rescued and cared for. The subtle expressions of the faces of Egielski's tub people help children understand how facial expressions communicate meaning.

Shirley Hughes. *Alfie Gives a Hand* (Lothrop, 1983). Shirley Hughes is a British writer, but the stories she tells are of the drama in the lives of young children in the United States. If you enjoy this storybook, you are sure to like her other tales of Alfie and his little sister Annie Rose, as well. In this book, Alfie overcomes his dilemma of being both excited and shy about going to his first birthday party at a friend's house. Children and adults will be charmed by the warmth of the pictures and the strong accounts of trust between adults and children that can be found in all of Shirley Hughes' work.

Don Freeman. *Corduroy* (Viking, 1968). This story about a teddy bear's adventurous trip through a department store, late at night, begins with a little girl named Lisa who sees him in the toy department and wants him for her own. Happily, the story ends with Corduroy going home with her.

FOLKTALES AND FAIRY TALES

These stories have been passed down to us primarily by being told rather than read. We often assume that children know stories such as "Little Red Riding Hood" or "Jack and the Beanstalk," but many of today's children have missed the opportunity to learn these traditional tales that some of us know by heart. Fortunately, many gifted writers and illustrators are retelling these tales for our children.

Suggested Reading

Jan Brett. *The Mitten: A Ukrainian Folktale* (Putnam, 1989). Brett's retelling of this tale about a lost mitten that gives shelter to an amazing number of animals, features beautiful paintings of a snow-covered landscape. Each page features a preview of what's to come, and so the book creates a great opportunity for talking to children about ideas from the pictures.

Paul Galdone. *The Three Little Pigs* (Clarion, 1970). Galdone's illustrations of this classic folktale of the little guy using his head to outwit the big guy, are just right for helping young listeners follow the story's action.

Eric Kimmel, reteller, and Megan Lloyd, illustrator. *The Gingerbread Man* (Holiday House, 1993). Even children who know this story well will enjoy Lloyd's detailed and realistic pictures, which will help children imagine this story happening at a farm just down the highway. They may also take note of Kimmel's addition to the story's end.

Patricia McKissack, author, and Rachel Isadora, illustrator. *Flossie and the Fox* (Dial, 1986). This variation on "Red Riding Hood" features an African-American girl who outsmarts the fox. This book's story line is more complicated than "Red Riding Hood," but it will be enjoyed by older preschoolers who are familiar with other folktales.

PLAY BOOKS

Some books are designed for children to play with as well as to tell a story. Pop-up, Scratch and Sniff, and Lift-the Flap books are examples of these. Of course such books require extra care, but children do enjoy them. In fact, children who are not yet interested in books, can often be steered into literature through enjoyable experiences with play books. Young children with attentional problems, or with sensory disabilities can often be drawn into stories more easily when we read books such as these.

We recommend that you use play books with children, but don't expect preschoolers to be unusually gentle with them. Have an adult be responsible for caring for these books. Make certain that an adult holds the book while it is read and that the book be stored away from unsupervised children's reaches in order to preserve its life.

Suggested Reading

Eric Carle. *The Very Hungry Caterpillar* (Philomel, 1987). This story of the caterpillar who eats one apple on Monday, two pears on Tuesday, and lots more on Wednesday through Sunday, has become a preschool classic. Children enjoy counting while touching the cutout holes that appear on each piece of food. Eric Carle's work includes additional books that involve children in listening to, touching, and folding out pages.

Tana Hoban. *Look! Look! Look!* (Greenwillow, 1988). Each beautifully photographed object in this book is presented first through a small circular hole, showing just one part. Children try to guess what the object is, then turn the page to see the whole picture. This is then followed by a view of the object from a distance. Once children know this book, they enjoy asking others to guess the pictures.

Paul O. Zelinsky. *The Wheels on the Bus* (Dutton, 1990). This book is a perfect depiction of that favorite song, with its moving parts for each verse: a door that opens and shuts, windows that go up and down, passengers that go bumpity-bump. You will hear lots of calls to "read it again."

WORDLESS BOOKS

These are actually storybooks, but the stories are told by the pictures. We "read" these books by reading the pictures. Unlike books with words, the wordless story will sound a bit different each time it is told. Because of this, children are eager to jump in and help tell what they see in the pictures. When reading a wordless book, point out to your listeners that the book has no words, and so you and the children will have to look closely at the pictures to find out what happens in the story. You will probably be surprised at how well preschoolers focus on important events in pictures. When children seem to miss something, you can ask questions to draw their attention to the story. The ability to "read" pictures will help word recognition skills when children are older.

Suggested Reading

Alexandra Day. *Carl Goes Shopping* (Farrar, 1989). This is one of a series of books whose main character is the amazing Rott-weiler, Carl. Since Rottweilers are guard dogs, Carl is often asked to watch the baby. Each story is full of adventures the baby experiences with fun-loving Carl. Children can't wait to turn the pages to see what Carl will do next. Carl always takes care of the baby, though, whether that means putting her down for a nap on a pile of rugs at the department store or finding her cookies and milk in the food department.

Pat Hutchins. *Changes, Changes* (Macmillan, 1971). This story is portrayed by wooden people with their block set. As the action unfolds, we see the people change the same set of blocks from a house into a firetruck, a boat, and back into a house. An added bonus in this book is that it gives children ideas of things they can create and role play with their own blocks.

Jan Ormerod. *Sunshine* (Lothrop, 1981). In this story a young girl is the first to rise at her house, and she helps her parents get up and off to work. Children will enjoy the fact that the girl seems a bit more awake and competent than her parents, as they burn toast and lose socks.

PREDICTABLE STORIES

Children are likely to join in as we read them these kinds of stories because they can figure out which words will come next. Sometimes this is because of rhyming words and sometimes because certain words or phrases are repeated. These are important books for preschoolers to experience, since they provide opportunities for pretending to read. When joining in, children practice saying words fluently and with expression, and they feel pride and joy in reading a book.

Suggested Reading

John Langstaff, reteller, and Nancy Winslow Parker, illustrator. *Oh, A-Hunting We Will Go.* (Atheneum, 1974). This humorous book is based on the folksong, with rhyming verse,

"We'll catch a fox and put him in a box. . . " John Langstaff, with help from some children, has devised many new verses to this song. The words and pictures will tickle children's funnybones ("We'll catch a bear and put him in underwear!") as they quickly learn to sing or chant this book.

Linda Williams, author, and Megan Lloyd, illustrator. *The Little Old Lady Who Was Not Afraid of Anything.* (Crowell, 1986). This cumulative tale is a perfect story for autumn, as it ends with the construction of a scarecrow. The little old lady finds herself followed by some clothing and accessories as she walks through the woods. Each item makes a particular noise and action, for example, "One shirt goes, 'Shake, Shake.'" Children easily learn the words and motions and the story can be followed by fall activities such as drawing or making a scarecrow or pumpkin head.

Sue Williams, author, and Julie Vivas, illustrator. *I Went Walking.* (Harcourt, 1989). In this story, a young child goes walking and sees several animals. The story uses a pattern of questions and answers throughout: "I went walking. What did you see? I saw a black cat looking at me." Children quickly learn to memorize the pattern and just check the pictures to name each new animal. The print is large, making this a good book for helping older preschoolers focus on letters or words. The illustrations are large and uncluttered, making it helpful for toddlers learning animal names.

CONCEPT AND INFORMATIONAL BOOKS

We sometimes think of these as books designed to teach children something, for example, the alphabet or numbers. However, the best of concept books do not directly teach concepts, but rather, present concepts within a storybook or other interesting format. Good concept books are enjoyable whether or not children actually take away or learn the particular concepts being presented. Young children can tell when books are "preachy" and when we are reading just to teach them something. As a result, they do not enjoy the story and the experience does not expand their enjoyment of books. Likewise, we have discovered that children who are exposed to good literature, soon learn to recognize it, and are not interested in listening to books that don't meet their standards.

What do we look for in suitable concept and information books? Here, certainly, we need to closely examine the illustrations. Are they easy to see? Are they realistic or, if not, are they presented in an artistic style appropriate for the words? Do they help children understand the concepts in the text? These are necessary characteristics. In addition, children enjoy photographs (especially of animals), they enjoy illustrations that include children and other people. When we examine the text, we try to find books that can explain concepts without using too many words, and that use words children can easily understand.

Finally, be certain that you have a range of informational books available for your children: books about colors, numbers, letters, people, animals, machines, history, seasons, art, music, etc. We want to expose children to a broad range of ideas.

Suggested Reading

Joanna Cole, author, and Margaret Miller, photographer. *My Puppy is Born.* (Morrow, 1991). Large colored photographs and a small amount of text tell the story of a little girl's new dog from the time the mother dog is pregnant until Dolly is eight weeks old and can go home with the child. We see the little girl interacting with her new puppy in many of the pictures. Children will learn about how puppies learn as well as how they grow, and how to take care of a puppy's emotional needs as well as physical needs.

Shirley Hughes. *Giving.* (Candlewick, 1993). In this book, Hughes introduces children to an important social concept, giving. Each page shows one aspect of giving, and includes positive (a slice of apple), as well as negative (an angry look) gifts. The pictures portray familiar events in the lives of young children. As with all Hughes' work, the book is a warm, loving picture of childhood.

Shirley Hughes. *Lucy and Tom's A.B.C.* (Viking, 1986). Shirley Hughes is a master at telling a story while teaching and her stories are told as exquisitely through her pictures as her words. Children will pour over the illustrations and relish the words. Lucy is a preschooler, and her brother Tom, a toddler. Readers learn about Lucy and Tom's world while being introduced to words that begin with the letters a, b, etc. What a delightful way to lead children to think about the alphabet.

Eve Merriam, author, and Eugenie Fernandes, illustrator. *Daddies at Work* and *Mommies at Work.* (Simon & Schuster, 1989). How children love to look at these pages, to find people like their own Mommies and Daddies, as well as their friends and relations. Information about one's own life and family is among the most important for preschoolers. Books like these remind children that literature is often about people just like them—we read to find ourselves.

Stephen Shott, photographer. *The World of the Baby* and *El Mundo del Bebe*. (Dutton, 1990). This first encyclopedia, appears in both English and Spanish versions. It is divided into important categories for babies: clothing, getting dressed, pets, foods, bath time. The photographs are striking, clear, and a delight to the eyes. This will probably be a browsing book, where you and your child will take turns pointing to pictures saying, "What's that?"

REFERENCES

Butler, D., and Clay, M. 1985. *Reading begins at home.* Portsmouth, NH: Heinemann.

Durkin, D. 1966. *Children who read early.* New York: Teachers College Press.

Taylor, D., and Strickland, D. 1986. *Family storybook reading.* Portsmouth, NH: Heinemann.

Teale, W.H. 1984. "Reading to Young Children: Its Significance for Literacy Development" in *Awakening to literacy: The University of Victoria symposium on children's response to a literate environment: Literacy before schooling.* Goelman, H., Oberg, A.A. & Smith, F. (Eds.) Portsmouth, NH: Heinemann.

4 SETTING UP THE STORYBOOK CORNER IN LIBRARIES AND EARLY CHILDHOOD CENTERS

At first glance, one would think the job here consists of merely finding a relatively quiet corner, stocking it with good books, and making it cozy and bright. Indeed, that is a big part of the task, but let's consider some of the ways children use the storybook corner as well as ways we would like them to use it.

PURPOSES

Nearly every public library has a children's section or room devoted to books for children. Within that space, picture storybooks intended for the youngest of children play a featured role. Ideally, these books sit on shelves that a toddler can reach in a carpeted space with plenty of light, air, and color. Pint-sized chairs encourage independent "reading" for even the youngest patrons. Comfortable space for a child to share a favorite book with a parent or caregiver is nearby. The books themselves should be shelved as accurately as possible for the adult who is looking for a particular book, but not so strictly that parents need to constantly nag the child who loves to sample lots of different books but returns them to slightly different locations. Some libraries have conceded that the best solution is to keep all the books by B authors together, but not in any particular alphabetical order, since that is how they end up at the end of a busy day, anyway. The ideal storybook corner invites all children to partake in what it has to offer. Those colorful jackets and assorted shapes should be as magnetic as the candy in a sweetshop. Whether they look at twenty books to pick the right one or direct their moms to ask the librarian for their favorite book on boats, pigs, or "the blue one," the major purpose of any storybook area is achieved by promoting a love of books in children and providing a place to indulge that love.

In preschool, children use the storybook corner and books for some very personal reasons throughout their day. They use the area and its books for comfort. Children who aren't feeling well often gravitate to this area. It is a place where they can lie down, be quiet, and look at something familiar. For children who have a difficult time when Mom or Dad leaves them at school, hearing the parent read one story at school just before leaving can be a very calming routine to help in the transition, like a bedtime story. Children who arrive at preschool after having had a difficult morning (maybe an argument with a parent or sibling, maybe just too hectic a start) often choose the storybook corner as well. For some children this is one place where they don't have to interact with one another, or even with an adult. It becomes a private area where they can safely stay until they feel like interacting. Other children use the storybooks as a way to initiate contact with an adult. This is especially true when they have teachers who almost always say, "yes," to the request, "Will you read this to me?" When children want to sit in a lap, snuggle, laugh with someone, or otherwise get some special attention, they often bring the teacher or caregiver a book to read to them. In all these cases, the storybook corner fulfills a real need for the children. We have to be certain that we plan the area so that it continues to fulfill these purposes.

Preschool teachers rely on the Storybook Corner for many purposes, too. We use it to encourage all of our children to want to become readers! We want children to choose to go there during their free time. We want them to take time to pour over books, to notice the pictures and the print, and to remember storylines. We want them to return again and again to the storybooks we read at storytime, to remember the stories, and to develop their own favorites. We want them to learn, on their own, that books can make them laugh, give them something to talk with a friend about, and answer their questions.

GUIDELINES FOR LIBRARIES

Libraries can't always provide the ideal space for young children to gather with their books. Sometimes they are constrained by the lack of space and the need to serve all ages. Sometimes the building design stands in the way of a suitable arrangement. However, it is so important to recognize that of all the age groups a library serves, the preschoolers are the patrons most in need of high quality service. An adult who doesn't find a particular mystery novel may try another author or title, but a young child can't turn to anything else without a firm foundation in literacy.

Preschoolers don't vote or pay taxes. They don't fill out opinion surveys or make suggestions. They are often thought about by library administrators in terms of circulation desk coverage during preschool storytimes or when adult patrons complain they are making too much noise. Children's rooms are often in basements, not because it is the ideal space, but that it was as far away as they could be placed. Children's librarians sometimes find themselves justifying the importance of their work to librarians who find no need to justify the importance of their reference services to adults. The first step a library must take in serving preschool children well, is to proclaim the importance of young patrons in all library business — from building design, to policy formation, to administrative equity, to the simplest circulation transaction.

ADVOCACY FOR CHILDREN

1. Children's librarians must be advocates for all the patrons they serve, from babies through young adults, as well as their caregivers, teachers, and parents. Preschool children deserve special attention because of their inability to speak for themselves. Advocacy includes making certain that administrative policies do not discriminate against children developmentally. A "No Sleeping" rule in a public library not only targets an exhausted homeless person, presumably the purpose of such a discriminatory rule, but also would require babies to put off their naps until they are out of the building. Rules against running discriminate against toddlers who find that to be their normal mode of transportation. Rules against loud talking discriminate against the preschooler who is just months away from learning to truly whisper. Advocacy means representing the preschooler's library rights before the administration and public. Advocacy means speaking up on behalf of the youngest patrons who would express their needs if they could.

2. Advocacy also means that children's librarians must keep the matter of literacy an integral part of all aspects of library service to preschool children. The overall mission of providing an environment in which preschool children learn to love books should guide most decisions in collection development and program planning. If a single library visit makes a child wish to

return, a life-long habit is ready to begin. Wherever possible, make the use of the library easy for parents and children. Library card registration should begin at birth. Why say no to a parent who proudly requests a library card application for his one-week-old daughter? We have observed four-year-old children who are far more conscientious about caring for and returning their books than many 40-year-old patrons. Drop as many administrative road blocks to literacy as you possibly can.

3. Beyond the physical attractiveness of the space provided for children, a library needs to demonstrate a welcoming psychological space. Administrative support of public service training for all staff who face children is a must. Often, the circulation librarian delivers the first (and lasting) impression of the library to a young child and his caregiver. A welcoming smile can be a powerful first step in satisfying a parent and giving comfort to a child in a strange environment.

4. Administrative respect for children's services needs to be cultivated by children's librarians so that the entire staff can see the commitment to children's services. One of the best ways to demonstrate the importance of children's services is for children's librarians to demonstrate *their* importance in all aspects of library services. Children's librarians who volunteer for policy formation committees, keep up with technical services issues and electronic access innovations, and participate in management seminars or total quality management committees are more likely to earn the respect of the administration and their immediate colleagues. They will also become more knowledgeable children's librarians. And remember, since it is unlikely the children's librarian's colleagues will be studying child development or storytelling at the same time, the increase in knowledge and experience will very likely result in a stronger administrative voice and more clout for the children's librarian. The beneficiaries will be the preschool patrons whose "views" will be heard by people more capable of making decisions affecting day-to-day library service.

5. Children's librarians need to be knowledgeable about children's development. They must answer questions about why children behave the way they do and suggest books for nearly every purpose imaginable. A children's librarian who can demonstrate the connection between child development milestones and the objectives for storytime has built-in justification for the absolute necessity and value of that storytime.

6. Children's librarians need to model the behaviors they would like to see in others who come into contact with the children

in the library. "Showing" is nearly always more powerful than "telling." This not only includes the times when a children's librarian is separating fighting children or diplomatically attempting to silence two chatting parents during toddler time, but it also includes what happens away from the storytime. It might be a situation where a lost child is comforted and the librarian attempts to learn about the location of the missing parent in a quiet, non-threatening manner. It might be the positive comment a children's librarian adds about a hard-to-manage child who is being disparaged by adults or the silent rise and departure of the children's librarian from a conversation that turns to gossip about a particular family. Much can be learned about the positive ways we need to treat children from watching a talented children's librarian treat children and their caregivers positively.

7. Children's librarians must always remember the underserved populations in their communities, whether they consist of the day care children who cannot come to the library during the day and require personal visits, children who could come to a preschool storytime if it were held in the evening or on a Saturday morning, or children who live too far from the nearest branch and have no transportation. Not everyone is fortunate enough to have a parent who is able to bring him or her to the library. Outreach to the underserved must be a part of every preschool library service philosophy. How we can get kids to the library who have never been through the doors and how we can find and visit the rest are the two questions children's librarians must ask themselves on a regular basis.

BROWSING ARRANGEMENTS

1. A storybook area in a library needs to be many things to many people. Parents or caregivers wish to look for titles in a card or electronic catalog in close proximity to where their children will be browsing or reading. Children choose a variety of postures and positions in which to look at their books. Some like a chair in the corner—one that they just fit. Others like to sit on a "grown-up" chair at a table. Still others prefer soft bean bag chairs or lying on the floor. Ideally, as many difference preferences or styles as possible should be accommodated. *Proximity of catalog to collection* and *comfort for examining* the books are the two prime considerations. Having a slightly private space off to one corner is often appreciated by nursing mothers who can keep an eye on the older sibling while still having a bit of privacy. A changing table in a library is rare,

but appreciated mightily by the parent who has one or more in diapers. Having the children's librarian's desk nearby is also a help to the parent whose hands are full of the demands of childhood.

2. Displays should promote children's literature appropriate for the age groups meant to be in the picture storybook area. Commercial posters from publishers should be of books appropriate for the preschool audience and owned by the library, preferably more than one copy. Use of three dimensional objects familiar to children, such as toys and stuffed animals, displayed so that two- and three-year-old children can see them is encouraged. Having some displayed items available for petting or handling is so appreciated by the youngest crowd. Colorful mobiles, both commercial and homemade, are a good way to brighten the book area, tie the decorations to the collection, and to preserve the life of the decoration by hanging it out-of-reach of the children. Physical objects that tie into a storytime theme or a particularly popular story are great ways to keep preschoolers talking to their parents about what they heard or saw.

3. Handouts and booklists should be near the picture books, placed at the eye level of the adult caregivers. A few carefully considered publications are more helpful than hundreds of flyers for parents to sort through. Only display items of special relevance for parents or caregivers of preschoolers. Keep the community bulletin board somewhere else in the library.

4. A collection of parent/teacher/caregiver material nearby is especially helpful for parents who are wishing to browse adult material while their children are looking at storybooks. This can also be useful for parents who are keeping one eye on storytime and still hoping to do a little book browsing. One public library created a collection of material especially helpful to parents and caregivers on dozens of topics related to children and placed them together on an A-frame bookshelf next to the storybooks. A bibliography was available on the end of the shelf, so an adult could take the list home and plan what to seek on the next visit. Some of the material was available in the adult collection on the other side of the building, but the point was to gather material regarding children for the convenience of the parent, caregiver, or teacher who was present with children who were using the library.

STORYTIME SPACE

1. Having a storytime space in close proximity to the books themselves makes sense, but not so close that children can reach over and pull books off the shelf during the storytime. Soft carpeting is the best seating for preschoolers with some chairs in the back for use by caregivers or parents with younger children.

2. The children's librarian should ideally be backed into the corner looking out at where latecomers will arrive behind the audience. This gives the librarian visual control of the room and at least a chance to have the program fairly compete with the noise of a late arrival. Avoid sitting in front of windows unless shades or blinds can be drawn. If possible, sitting in front of a light colored wall or screen allows the colors of the books and materials being presented a chance to leap out at the children. Having the librarian elevated places the preschoolers in an approximation of a theater seating. A child-sized chair or low stool works well for four- and five-year-olds, while sitting directly on the floor might work best with toddlers. Making a presentation at the audience's height while still allowing all to see is the goal.

3. Display other books on the same topic or by the same authors and illustrators somewhere along the path between the storytime area and the circulation desk. This is a good strategy for promoting follow-up reading (and book circulation).

4. Some storytimes, especially those designed for babies and toddlers, include parents or caregivers in an active, hands-on role. Many older preschool storytimes allow for parents to watch, but do not have a specific role designed for the adults. It is as important to have something for those parents to do during the storytime as it is to have something for their children to do when the parents are checking out the books at the circulation desk. Have interesting material to look at quite handy, especially book collections such as the parent/teacher/caregiver collection mentioned earlier. For children at the circulation desk, a wipable board with a pen/marker hanging on a string could provide just the right entertainment for the three minutes the children wait for their parents. Perhaps just a chair or two with their little backs against the base of the circulation desk would do the trick? Having a child-sized circulation area with a desk cut low for a child to assist in checking out

his or her own books often works wonders in smoothing the post-storytime process. Taking a cue from the candy displays at grocery store cash registers, how about an adult paperback rack near the storytime space for the parents, and a children's paperback rack by the circulation desk?

GUIDELINES FOR EARLY CHILDHOOD CENTERS

Keeping both children's and teacher's purposes in mind, let us consider some guidelines for setting up a storybook area in a preschool or child care center.

PHYSICAL ARRANGEMENTS

1. Make sure the area is large enough to seat five or six children and one adult. The area should hold five to six times more books than you have children. This may seem like a lot of books, 75 for 15 children, but this allows ample choice for children at times when nearly everyone is looking at books. With this many books, we can more readily provide for the variety of books suggested in Chapter 3.
2. Make the area attractive and inviting. Use bright colors; decorating with book jackets or posters depicting reading or storytelling. Maintain children's interest by periodically changing displays and book arrangements.
3. Young children can find books best when they are displayed facing out on racks or on shelves. Try to avoid traditional spine-out library shelving when you are able to.
4. Put soft pillows, beanbag chairs, carpeting squares, stuffed animals, and dolls in the area. This is especially important when children are there seeking comfort.
5. Make certain that the storybook corner is in a quiet area of the room, without a lot of pass-through traffic. We want children to be able to hear well, to talk with the reader, and to be undistracted.
6. *But,* don't make it so secluded that it becomes a forgotten, "out-of-the-way" spot. We want parents to browse its shelves. We want children to see it *everytime* they are wondering what to do. We want to communicate its importance by giving it an

important space in the classroom. Consider placing it near the area where you conduct your storytime so children can see you return books to the shelves.

7. In addition to having a special reading or storytime area, remember to make the other areas of the center "print rich" as well, so reading and word play are not isolated from other activities. For example, have some books on colors and crafts available in the art activities area.

THE BOOK COLLECTION

1. About every two to four weeks, put away about one-third of your collection, replacing them with new books. In a child care center where children have many opportunities to look at the books, every two weeks is appropriate. In a half-day preschool program, a longer period will probably be needed for children to spend adequate time with the books. Children's interest will be sparked regularly by the appearance of new books.

2. Include non-traditional print in the area also, for example an occasional newspaper (telling about the recent blizzard!), bound copies of group or individual experience stories, relevant magazines, and travel brochures. We often place one volume of an encyclopedia in the storybook corner, marking a page that is of current interest to the children (e.g., polar bears during a unit on cold-weather animals). Children do enjoy perusing such a large "book of knowledge." We make book markers that have pictures on top so that children can refer to the pictures to find the appropriate pages.

3. Try always to have some multiple copies of a favorite book. Young children enjoy sitting with a friend, showing, talking about, and finding the same pages together—demonstrating what a true social event reading can be!

4. When you move books in and out of the collection, be certain that old favorites make periodic return trips. There will probably be some books that the children will insist on keeping for months.

5. Place seasonal and holiday readings in the collections. Literature is a great way to anticipate and celebrate the changing world around us.

6. If possible, provide a listening center with stories read on tape by the teacher or a favorite storyteller.

7. Place related toys, puppets, and storytelling kits in the area periodically. These will help children tell as well as read the stories. For example, a wolf puppet will likely help a child tell "The Three Pigs" with great drama.

MANAGING THE STORYBOOK CENTER

1. Remember that it is *repeated* book experiences that lead to many discoveries about reading. Children need the opportunity to hear the same story read again and again—the opportunity to satisfy their desires to study the pictures, the opportunity to have some of the print pointed out time and time again ("This big word is the one that says, 'HELP'")—in order to have storybook reading lead to learning about print. So think about how you can provide repeated reading opportunities for children. The following ideas may help:

   - Make certain that you and your helpers have read every book in the collection aloud to the children at least once.
   - Allow children to check out books from the classroom collection. They are usually most anxious to have a parent read them a story they already enjoyed in school.
   - When you put out new books, show them to the children at story time, thereby giving them "sneak previews" of the books and motivating them to read and look at them.
   - Arrange for volunteer readers, listeners, or storytellers (retired persons, older children, parents) to come regularly and spend time in the storybook center.
   - Make certain that sometimes, in the day, children can choose the storybook you will read.

2. Teach children how to take care of books by modeling book care yourself. When you take out and replace books from the shelves, talk aloud about how you are doing it ("I want to be sure this is all the way back so it doesn't fall.").

3. After children have had opportunities to learn about book care from you, have a book care discussion and make a chart or booklet with the children's ideas in it. In the future you can refer to these when children need reminding. They will need reminders (so be prepared to do it patiently) as they tend to treat books as toys.

4. This brings us to the notion of books as toys: young children *do* play with books, and that is a positive thing. In fact they learn much about books through play. They pretend to be a parent or teacher, and "read" to their friends or dolls. They put their fingers under words, point to pictures, in general they pretend to read. Many children are content to do their pretend reading in the storybook corner. Others will want to take books to the housekeeping area (after all, their babies are there!) or to the pretend doctor's office. Certainly these are

appropriate ways to play with books. Be very specific about your rules for this, however. You may want children to ask before taking books to other areas, or have a rule about which books may be used for this, etc.

5. Categorize some books within your collection, so that children can find what they are looking for; and so they begin to think about the various characteristics of books. There are many ways to do this. You can keep all very small or large books together. Keep music books, poetry books, or wordless books together. Keeping all unit-related books together on a special shelf or in a special box is helpful. If you are focusing on the work of one author or illustrator, you could keep these books in a separate space. Don't do all of this at once (we don't want children to think of this as a sorting chore), but perhaps only one or two separate categories at a time.

6. If your center has limited funds for its book collection, try some of these ideas: buy paperbacks, join a book club, shop at yard-sales and library sales, borrow an extended loan collection from your public library, suggest the book collection as a fund-raising goal for your families or an interested community organization.

In summary, we need to see the storybook corner as an important area of focus, one that serves a variety of needs, one that requires regular upkeep and constant replacement.

5 PLANNING FOR STORYTIMES

The storytime is a highlight of library programming for children and an important focus of preschool programs as well. For children, this is an opportunity to come together in a group, get to know one another, and share literacy experiences and ideas with each other and adults. For adults, this is an opportunity to help direct and focus the children's attention toward particular literacy activities. In preschool settings, the storytime sometimes includes more than "story" activities. It might include calendar time, morning greetings, and talking about the day's activities. We suggest, however, that these other activities be kept to a minimum. Research shows that when children are in a group or circle time, they pay best attention to the stories, songs, and rhymes while encountering the most difficulty in paying attention to routine activities such as calendar, review, and show-and-tell (McAfee, 1985). You will notice that we are using "storytime" to denote a wide range of literature-related activities often referred to as "storyhour." Realizing that storyhour implies a certain length of time, often impossible to find in a center, and usually inappropriately long for preschool-aged children, we have chosen to use the more functional term.

HELPFUL HINTS FOR PLANNING STORYTIMES

When we try to incorporate too many other activities into storytimes, we make it harder for children to pay attention, and harder for adults to keep children's attention. We lessen children's learning and everyone's enthusiasm. Since our purpose is to help children get the most from their experiences with literature, we recommend an approach that centers on stories, rhymes, and music; keeping other activities to a minimum. In the plans and outlines for storytimes provided in this chapter, we follow this approach. Each plan takes about 25 to 40 minutes to carry out, depending on how long you spend on the craft or activity, how much discussion takes place, and how many times you repeat the songs and rhymes. We suggest that you adapt these plans to the special needs of the group of children with which you work, taking into consideration their attention abilities and other skills. For example in a child care setting, you might choose to take a break (playtime, snack) between the story and an accompanying activity.

When planning for your own storytimes, we suggest you keep some guidelines in mind. First, of course, review developmental information concerning the age group with which you are working. The tables in chapter one provide a summary of children's developing abilities and pointers for how adults can support this development. In addition to this we offer the following guidelines:

- Develop a sequenced outline of activities that you will adhere to for each storytime so that children can learn and anticipate the routine. For example, in our Toddler Storytime plans, we start with an introduction, followed by two songs or rhymes, then present the story, do a project or craft, and end by repeating one of the songs or rhymes.
- Develop some clear routines to signal the beginning and the end of the storytime. Again, in our Toddler plans, we begin with a welcoming song, and end with a goodbye song.
- Try to include something (song, rhyme, or story) familiar in each of your programs. This serves two purposes: children pay better attention to the familiar, and they are reminded that they already know some good literature.
- Practice the reading or telling of the story, as well as the singing and chanting of the rhymes, so that you feel comfortable enough to glance only periodically at the words. When working with children, your eyes will need to be on the audience most of the time.
- Perform all of the literature (song, rhyme, story) with enthusiasm and whole-hearted enjoyment. An important part of this experience is teaching children that literature really is wonderful! Enjoyment is the key to the habit of lifelong reading.
- When reading stories, be certain the children can all see the pictures, and have time to think about and enjoy them. Visual literacy is important.
- Before reading the story, draw children into it by relating it to their experiences — with older preschoolers by asking them questions.
- Do whatever is necessary to help children understand the story. Sometimes this means repeating an important phrase,

asking a question, or saying something in another way.

- Allow children to ask questions as you read, since this helps them understand and personalize stories. If you sense the questions are leading others away from the story, indicate time for more questions at the end.
- Repeat new songs or poems at least twice so that children have a chance to learn them. Periodically send home copies of these, so that parents can learn them too. If they don't learn them, at least they will understand what their children are saying!
- Help children pay attention throughout the program by including opportunities for them to participate and move about (even standing up to sing some songs, moving to another area to complete the craft or activity).
- If children check out books after the story period, try to gather other interesting books related to the story theme, and if possible provide extra copies of the featured book for them to check out.

The rest of this chapter contains several examples of storytimes. We present some complete plans as well as ideas for others (Starter Plans). They are presented in two sections. The first section includes plans that are appropriate for two- and three-year-olds. These will also be useful for older children who have had limited experiences in group storytimes, or who have difficulty paying attention during group time. The second section of plans are for older three-, four-, and five-year-olds. We have used all the complete and starter plans ourselves, and so we can attest to children's enjoyment of them. We suggest, however, that you look at all of the plans as ideas for you to adapt for your own particular setting.

STORYTIME PLANS FOR TODDLERS OR BEGINNING LISTENERS

Each of these plans begins and ends with a song:

Welcome Song
[sung to tune, "Did You Ever See a Lassie?"]

We all are here for story time, story time, story time.
We all are here for story time; to have some fun!

Ending Song
[sung to tune, "If You're Happy and You Know It."]

If you had fun today and you know it, clap your hands.
If you had fun today and you know it, clap your hands.
If you had fun today and you know it, then your face will surely
show it.
If you had fun today and you know it, clap your hands.

[sing next verse, if book check-out follows]

If you're ready to get a book now, wave goodbye.
If you're ready to get a book now, wave goodbye.
If you're ready to get a book, then you'd better take a look.
If you're ready to get a book now, wave goodbye.

PLAN 1
Topic: Owls at Night

1. Welcome Song.
2. Introduce nighttime theme by pretending it is nighttime, have children pretend to get in their beds, look out windows and sing, "Twinkle, Twinkle Little Star."
3. Have children stand up, pretend to look out their windows at nighttime. Teach them to act out this poem:

Three Little Owls

Three little owls without any home,
[hold up three fingers]

Three little trees in a row.
[hold up three fingers, other hand, holding arm higher]

Come build your nests,
[with "tree fingers," motion to come]

In our branches tall,
[make owls fly up to trees]

We'll rock you to and fro.
[join all fingers and rock with arms]

4. Present storybook: *Owl Babies* by Martin Waddell. Although this book has beautiful illustrations, children also enjoy it when presented as a felt board story. If you choose to make a felt set, it can be done simply, by making a tree, a moon, the mother owl, and the three baby owls. Placing them on a black flannel board creates a lovely nighttime picture. A large owl puppet

or stuffed animal to represent the mother owl is also good for capturing children's attention. You can make that mother owl fly over the children on her way home.

5. *Activity:* Make Owl Puppets from brown paper bags. You will need to precut eyes, ears, and beaks which children can glue on their puppets. They can color the body of the owls, or you can purchase feathers for gluing at a craft store. Toddlers who are recently gaining control of the pincer grasp, love picking up the various pieces and placing them on top of the glue.

6. When owls are complete, and you have complimented them, asked about the owls' names, etc., call children back together so their owls can pretend to look out of their trees and help the children sing, "Twinkle, Twinkle, Little Star."

7. Goodbye Song.

PLAN 2
Topic: A Great Surprise!

1. Welcome Song.
2. Tell the children that the surprise today has to do with someone's birthday, that they will be hearing a story about a birthday. Surely they will have some things to tell you themselves by this time—"I had a birthday," "I'm three," etc. Show children a picture of a birthday cake or, if you are able, bring along a real cake to eat later. Have children help you act out the stages of making a birthday cake—putting in various ingredients, stirring, putting batter in a pan, baking, spreading icing. Then teach them the following rhyme:

Birthday Candles

Today I have a birthday.
I'm four-years-old, you see.
[hold up four fingers]

And here I have a birthday cake,
[bring arms together in circle]
Which you may share with me.
[point to others in group]

First we count the candles,
[hold up pointer finger]
Count them everyone.

One, two, three, four,
[hold up fingers as count]
The counting now is done.

Let's blow out the candles.
[point to lips]
Out each flame will go.

Wh. . . Wh. . . Wh. . . Wh. . .
[pretend to blow candles]
As one by one we blow.
[starting with pinkie, bend each finger down as you blow]

3. Tell children that the story begins with a Mommy's birthday, so let's sing the "Happy Birthday to You" song. If parents are along, have children sing the birthday song to their parents.

4. Tell or read children the story, *The Surprise* by George Shannon. In this story, a baby animal decides to send his mother a surprise package for her birthday. After opening several nested packages, the mother finds her own child inside the last one. All children are curious about what's inside packages, so wrap up some packages yourself to open when you get to the end of this story. You will need three stuffed animals for this story, one mother and two babies (so one can be inside the package while the other is used for acting out the story). Then you will need boxes which fit inside each other, and wrapping paper.

5. *Activity:* Give children playdough which they can use to make a cake, complete with candles. Allow children a chance to experiment with or play with the playdough a bit before you encourage them to make a birthday cake. When you do so, make a cake yourself, pointing out how you make a ball (roll "round and round"), and "pat, pat" it down to make the cake. Then roll some snake shapes for candles. Try counting out four candles as in the poem, but don't insist that children do this. You may wish to let children take their playdough home to show their family their cake-making ability, or to remind them about storytime. If you are working with four- and five-year-olds, they would enjoy gift wrapping their playdough (maybe double-or triple wrapping it as in the story). It's great fun for them to work with gift wrap and tape!

6. While children are coming to the end of the playdough activity, and some have the cakes they've made, repeat the poem or the singing of "Happy Birthday to You."

7. Goodbye Song.

Playdough Recipe

This is a cooked version that cleans up easily and lasts for weeks. Makes enough for ten children doing this project.

1 cup flour
1 tablespoon oil
1 cup water
1/2 cup salt
2 teaspoons cream of tartar
food coloring is optional

Combine ingredients, cook over medium heat, stirring constantly. When the mixture forms a ball in the middle of pan (consistency of mashed potatoes), remove from the heat and knead for a few minutes. If mixture is still wet, return to heat to dry more. Store covered.

PLAN 3
Topic: A Trip to the Farm

1. Welcome Song.
2. Tell the children that, today, they will be taking a trip to a farm. Ask who has been to a farm? Ask what animals they might see there? Tell them to get ready, they will be going on a bus. Sing "The Wheels on the Bus." Add some farm fun to the trip, having children open the windows as you get closer:

   "The windows on the bus go Up and Down."

   "The cows in the meadow go MOO, MOO, MOO."

   "The mower on the farm goes Snip, Snip, Snip"
   [spread fingers, move apart and together]

   "The plow on the farm goes Scrape, Scrape, Scrape"
   [cup hands together and push forward]

3. Pretend to get off the bus at the farm, pointing out that you will soon be meeting some animals. Show some farm animal models or stuffed animals, asking children what noises they make. Then sing an animal-sound song. You might choose "Old

MacDonald" or "Cat Went Fiddle-i-Fee." The words and music to this last song are featured in the lovely picture book, *Fiddle-i-Fee by* Melissa Sweet.

4. Read the book, *The Big Red Barn* by Margaret Wise Brown, using the Big Book version illustrated by Felicia Bond. Make a three-dimensional barn by covering a cardboard box with paper and adding a door and a removable roof. If you have any stuffed or model farm animals, put them inside to be taken out at the appropriate time in the story. Children will enjoy playing with these props afterwards, too. It will give you a chance to use words such as *inside, outside, beside, big,* and *small* with the children as they play.

5. *Activity:* Make paper plate animal masks with crayons, precut pieces, and glue. Have three or four animals that children can choose from. When children are finished, have them come back to the circle to look at two or three pages of the book again, acting out the story events with their masks on. Some good choices are the pages that show the animals "making funny noises," playing "all day in the grass and in the hay," and "all night long sound asleep."

6. Sing the animal sounds song again, or (if you've already heard enough animal sounds) put animal masks back in the barn, say goodbye to the farm, get back on the bus, and sing "Wheels on the Bus" in the reverse direction.

7. Goodbye Song.

STORYTIME STARTER PLANS FOR BEGINNING LISTENERS

1. *The Very Hungry Caterpillar* by Eric Carle as featured story. Make felt board set to accompany telling of the story. Pieces can easily be drawn from the bold pictures in the book. Children enjoy using them after the story, getting experience in counting and naming foods, and using concepts big and little.

   Find songs/rhymes about caterpillars, food, or butterflies. Make butterflies with crayons and construction paper. Glue them to clothespins so children can fly them around. Or, make caterpillars with toilet paper rolls or egg crate segments.

   Many puppetry shops sell a caterpillar that, when turned inside out, becomes a butterfly.

A favorite children's action-song about caterpillars is "Little Arabella Miller" sung to the tune of "Twinkle, Twinkle Little Star."

> Little Arabella Miller
> found a woolly caterpillar.
> [pretend to pick up one]
> First it crawled up on her mother,
> [creep finger up arm]
> then it crawled up on her brother.
> [creep up other arm]
> They said, "Arabella Miller,
> [shake finger angrily]
> take away that caterpillar!"
> [pretend to throw away]

2. *Jump, Frog, Jump!* by Robert Kalan as featured story. Try to obtain Scholastic's Big Book version of the story, and a frog (bean bag, puppet, stuffed toy) that you can make jump toward the children at the appropriate times while you read the story. Have children join in the chant, "Jump, Frog, Jump."

   Find rhymes/songs about frogs or other plants and animals found at a pond. For an activity, make frog masks so children can act out role of the frog, or play a catching game using the bean bag frog.

3. *Mouse Paint* by Ellen Walsh as featured story. Young children enjoy the bright pictures and find the language repeatable. We suggest bringing an easel with red, yellow, and blue paints to the story area so that you can create some of the story's colorful happenings as you read.

   Poems and songs about mice or colors will fit well here. Try the poem, "Mice" by Rose Fyleman, found in a Big Book of poetry (*Animals on Parade*). This story begs for a finger-painting follow up, with children using their fingers to make tracks, to mix colors.

Finger Paint Recipe:

2/3 cups boiling water
1 tablespoon glycerin
1 cup Ivory Soap Flakes
Several drops food coloring
Stir and thicken until clear, boiling only one minute.

---

4. *Now We Can Go* by Ann Jonas as featured book. You can act out this whole story with a doll, a toy box, a bag, and some toys. The story involves a lot of taking out and putting in, a favorite pastime of toddlers. Poems and songs about toys, cleaning up, or going on a trip would fit nicely. A follow-up activity in which children play or make a home-made game would give children more practice in throwing to or dropping into a target, using concepts inside and outside. Toys can be made with food canisters (oatmeal boxes) and clothespins or spools. If you use spools, add string so that they can become a stringing game, too. Old nylons rolled into a ball can be used for throwing into a large food canister.

5. *The Gingerbread Man* as a featured story. We suggest the version retold by Eric A. Kimmel and illustrated by Megan Lloyd because of its optimistic ending and the captivating personality Lloyd gives her Gingerbread Man. Children will certainly want to bake their own after the story. Older preschoolers can take their cookies home, and the next day dictate some adventures their own Gingerbread Men had.

    Rhymes and songs about baking, the sense of smell, running, and animals will fit this story nicely. Of course a chasing game or a guess-the-scent game would be appropriate also.

STORYTIME PLANS FOR PRESCHOOLERS

In our story hour sequence for preschoolers, we don't use songs to mark the beginning and end, yet you may still wish to do so. We prefer to begin with a topical introduction done by an adult or by a "host" puppet to set the tone of the storytime. We end with a summary involving discussion among children and the adult leader. In each of the plans that follow, the activity sequence goes as follows—an introduction, two rhymes/songs, story, activity/project, summary. We assume your audience already has group storytime experience so we don't always include a familiar song or rhyme as we did in the toddler plans.

PLAN 1
Storytime Theme: A Boat Trip
1. *Introduction:* Ask children to share some experiences in taking boat rides or with their toy boats in the tub.

2. Sing "Row, Row, Row Your Boat." On the second sing through, have children rock gently with the song, imagining a peaceful rowboat ride on a stream.

3. Ask if any of their toy boats have had accidents. Have they tipped over? Teach children the poem, "Belly and Tubs" by Clyde Watson from *Father Fox's Penny Rhymes*. Discuss how shouting and quarreling could cause a boat to tip over.

4. *Featured Story: Mr. Gumpy's Outing* by John Burningham. Children enjoy seeing this story acted out with toy animals and a boat. We use a puppet for Mr. Gumpy, a paper bag cut down and colored for his house, another for his boat, blue construction paper for the lake, and small stuffed animals to go along on the boat ride (don't worry if you don't have exactly the same ones as in the book).

   Introduce Mr. Gumpy who wants to take a gentle boat ride and do some fishing on his lake. Ask children if they think he will have a gentle ride or a ride like Belly and Tubs did. Tell or read the story.

5. *Activity:* We have two ideas here, a game and a craft.

   – Play a fishing game if you have a magnetic fishing pole set. Match fish as children catch them; matching colors, animal pictures, letters, or whatever would be appropriate for your children.
   – As a craft, cut cardboard milk cartons in half for boats. Have children make their own Mr. Gumpy's by coloring and adding paper scraps to toilet paper rolls. Glue stiff paper feet to each roll/Mr. Gumpy, so that it will stand up. Children can take their boats and their Gumpys home to play with, or play with them at school.

6. *Summary:* If you acted out the story with stuffed animals, have children help you review the sequence in which they got into the boat. Talk to children about toys they have at home that might fit in the boat with their Mr. Gumpys.

PLAN 2
Storytime Theme: A Windy, Spring Day

1. *Introduction:* Motivate children to think, play with, and talk about the wind by bringing in any of a variety of items that demonstrate air movement: electric fan, folded fan, pinwheel, air pump, birthday candles. Try to steer the discussion into some mention of wind that is helpful (drying clothes on clothes line) and wind that is harmful (tornado).

2. These two poems, which point out two characteristics of the wind, are fairly short. Both are found in *Sing a Song of Popcorn: Every Child's Book of Poems*.

- "Who Has Seen the Wind?" by Christina G. Rossetti. Have children listen as you recite this expressively; afterwards commenting on how we can't see wind, just its effects.
- "Wind Song" by Lilian Moore. Recite this expressively once, then ask children to accompany the words, acting-out (grasses swish, flags slap), and making sound effects (whisper, creak, hum).

3. Read *The Wind Blew* by Pat Hutchins. Give children lots of time to look at the illustrations, follow the accumulation of objects in the air, and appreciate the humor. Had you and the children considered that making us laugh is an example of how the wind is helpful?

4. *Activities:* (Two options)

- Make something that children can blow (a stiff paper pinwheel, a weather vane) or can use to move air (folded paper fan).
- If the weather has been windy and the grounds around your building have acquired some litter, why not go outside and collect some items the wind blew there. We usually need to limit the number of things each child can bring inside. When back inside, glue the items to a bulletin board or poster, labeling it, "Look What the Wind Blew!" This should follow the reading of Pat Hutchins' book.

5. *Summary:* Note how the wind brought us some good fun like Pat Hutchins' amusing story and pictures, our trip outside, or the craft project. If you happened to bring a fan for this storytime, children would enjoy a final laugh by saying, "Goodbye" into the fan's air stream, and listening to how it changes their voices.

PLAN 3
StorytimeTheme: Follow the Leader

1. *Introduction:* Start the storytime by having children stand up and follow you about the room doing what you do. After a short trip, return to the circle, and ask who knows the name of that game? Tell children that "Follow the Leader" will be the Storytime theme today.

2. Stand up again and sing and play together one of these imitational circle games: "Here We Go Round the Mulberry Bush," or "Did You Ever See a Lassie," or "Punchinello, Funny Fellow."

3. Recite and play the following rhyme, having children imitate you.

We Can Jump

"We can jump, jump, jump.
We can hop, hop, hop.
We can clap, clap, clap.
We can stop, stop, stop.
We can shake our heads for 'yes.'
We can shake our heads for 'no.'
We can bend our knees a little bit,
And sit down slow."

4. Read the story, *Do Like Kyla* by Angela Johnson. Ask children about their younger or older siblings, telling them that this story is about a big sister and a little sister. Show them the book cover, read the title, and ask if they can guess what the story might be about. After you read the story and look at the pictures, go back through it and suggest that the children take turns acting out some of the sequences.

5. Activity Suggestions:

- *Craft*—Make a mirror-image string painting. Pre-fold absorbent construction paper. Have children dip string into colored tempera paints. Have them squeeze out extra paint between their fingers as they pull the string out. Then lay the string in a pattern on the left side of the folded paper. Fold the blank side on top of the string, and press down (pull the string a bit while pressing, if you'd like movement in the pattern). Open up the picture, discard the strings, wet-wipe hands. Display the resulting pictures at summary time at the end of storytime.

- *Game*—Play a mirror buddy game. Use a full length mirror (from your dress-up corner) and demonstrate how our mirror images do just what we do. Then introduce the idea of "pretend mirrors," that we can pretend to be our buddy's mirror. Demonstrate by being the mirror image of one of the children, using simple motions such as raising a hand, a foot, leaning to one side. Pair up the children in mirror pairs.

6. *Summary:* Affirm the children's work by either having children show their pictures, or by reviewing some of the mirror actions you saw (remembering to use children's names as you recall).

PLAN 4
Storytime Theme: Care giving

1. *Introduction:* Ask children to share a bit about how they take care of their pets. Ask their thoughts on who takes care of wild animals. Accept all their ideas. Hopefully some will introduce ideas of mother and baby animals. Tell them that today's story is about a wild animal, a mouse.

2. Recite the poem, "Mice" by Rose Fyleman (poem and illustration found in the Big Book, *Animals on Parade*). Some children may tell you that they agree or disagree with this poem's notion that, "I think mice are rather nice." Tell them that the mouse in the story doesn't live in a house, and they will have to decide if they think she is a nice mouse while they hear the story. Note that only one poem or song is planned because the activity is lengthy.

3. Read *Henrietta's First Winter* by Rob Lewis. This is the story of a field mouse who has to go through her first winter all on her own (field mice don't live long, and her mother has died). She goes on to meet one misfortune after another in her efforts to store up food for the winter. Children will easily develop empathy for Henrietta, so stop periodically to ask how they think she is feeling, how we could help her.

4. *Activity:* Make a house for your own Henrietta. Note that depending on how much of this project the children do for themselves, it could take 30-40 minutes or be a two-day project.

    Each child will need a precut field mouse to color (use construction or other durable paper so their coloring doesn't tear the mouse). Children will also need a cut-down, brown paper lunch bag to cut fringe around.

    After children have colored their mice, fringed and folded down their mouse hole bags, they proceed to two stations already set up in the room. The first should contain items to make Henrietta's nest soft (cotton batting, Easter grass, shredded newspaper, old fabric scrap, whatever you have). The second should contain food items for Henrietta to store for winter (use paper or facsimiles for dried corn, beans, peas). Many preschool teachers prefer to keep real food out of activities other than meal or snack time.

    If you will miss music, why not sing as the children are

gathering up their nest items. Use the tune of "Way Down Yonder in the Paw-paw Patch" and sing: "Picking up grass and putting it in the nest," "Picking up peas and saving them for winter," and so on.

5. *Summary:* Glue a little note to each child's bag (note says, We read *Henrietta's First Winter* by Rob Lewis), as you compliment them on their cozy nests and ask them where they will keep their Henrietta when taking her home.

PLAN 5
Storytime Theme: ''Eat 'Em Up: Yum! Yum!''

1. *Introduction:* Begin by talking about foods we eat. What are some foods that are good for us? What are some foods that we like to eat, but aren't really healthy for us? Talk about how it is good for us to eat a lot of healthy foods and only a little bit of the others. We often use this story near Halloween since this is a way for children to think about working their Trick-or-Treat candies into daily life.

2. Pretend together that you are making a really healthy batch of pancakes, using whole wheat flour, raisins, and only a little bit of sugar. Then act out the following rhyme, ending by clapping hands together:

Pancake

Mix a pancake, stir a pancake,
Pop it in a pan.
Fry a pancake, toss a pancake,
Catch it if you can!

3. Sing a song about healthy food in a silly situation: "Aiken Drum" (sung by Raffi on "Singable Songs for the Very Young" or found in *Rise Up Singing: The Group-Singing Song Book).* Draw a moon outline and stick on or draw pictures of the various food/face parts as you sing about them. The children will quickly make their own silly suggestions for face parts.

Aiken Drum

There was a man lived in the moon, in the moon, in the moon.
There was a man lived in the moon and his name was Aiken
Drum.

And his hair was made of spaghetti, spaghetti, spaghetti,
And his name was Aiken Drum.

And his eyes were made of meatballs. . .

And his nose was made of cheese. . .

And his mouth was made of pizza. . .

4. Read the cumulative story, *The Fat Cat* by Jack Kent. Ask children to look at the cover of the book and share their ideas about why the cat is so fat.

   As you read the story, encourage the children to join in on the repeated lines, "My goodness, my little cat; what have you eaten, you are so fat!"

   We have made a puppet set to accompany the telling of this story (easily memorizeable since it rhymes). We used a pajama bag pattern to make a big orange cat. We used an opaque projector to enlarge pictures of the various characters that the cat eats, drawing them on muslin fabric. We used embroidery ink to draw in the features, then stuffed and sewed the characters. When telling the story, we feed each character into the cat, to the children's amazement. At the end of the story, we open up the cat as happens in the book, and out they all pop.

5. *Activity:* Play a food sorting game using pictures of healthy foods and other foods. Have children take turns reaching into a shopping bag, pulling out an empty food container or a picture of food to identify and to characterize as healthy or not. Have them place all the healthy foods in one area (top shelf of toy cupboard), and the other foods in another area (bottom shelf).

6. *Summary:* Recall the things that the cat ate, looking through the book, identifying them in order. Suggest that the children can probably "read/tell" this story to one another since they remember it so well.

PLAN 6
Storytime Theme: Bears

1. Remind children (hold up books, briefly ask about) of other bear stories they have read. Two stories especially related to this storytime are *Brown Bear, Brown Bear, What Do You See?* by Bill Martin Jr. and *We're Going On a Bear Hunt* by Michael Rosen. The featured book for this plan is patterned after *Brown Bear* and the activity is patterned after *We're Going on a Bear Hunt*. Preschoolers who have learned parts of these books "by heart" are delighted to recognize familiar components in the new story and activity, making this a very developmentally appropriate activity. Tell children that today's storytime is about

bears, and not just any bear, but Polar Bears. If you have a stuffed polar bear, use it as a prop.

2. Tell children that we will be searching for a bear today, in effect tracking a polar bear. Talk a bit about where a polar bear might be and what it might be doing. Then sing, "The Bear Went Over the Mountain."

3. Teach children the poem, "Polar Bear" by William J. Smith, acting it out as you chant it. After singing the song, mention that our bear might be sleeping on a cake of ice, too.

4. Read the story, *Polar Bear, Polar Bear What Do You Hear?* by Bill Martin, Jr.

5. Encourage children to join in as you read, perhaps going through the book a second time to help them learn the rhyme and story sequence. If they haven't already recognized the pattern from *Brown Bear, Brown Bear,* ask them if this reminds them of another bear story. Contrast seeing with hearing; the brown bear vs. the polar bear.

6. *Activity:* This is a polar bear hunt, patterned after the story, *We're Going on a Bear Hunt.* Typically the rhyme is chanted (in a call and response format) and accompanied by clapping with acting-out motions such as climbing a tree. In this activity, we actually set up a path for the bear hunt in the room (done ahead of time, complete with a hidden polar bear). Children can go on the hunt as they chant the rhyme. Practice the rhyme in the circle first. You may need to go through it twice so that children know the words well. Use the chanting scheme from Michael Rosen's book, using the following variations for the polar bear in the Arctic.

Refrain:

> We're going on a bear hunt,
> We're going to catch a big one.
> What a cold, beautiful day!
> We're not afraid.

Verse 1: (use egg crate foam covered with a green table cloth, for the squishy-squashy swamp)

> Oh! Oh! a mossy swamp
> A squishy-squashy, mossy swamp!

> We can't go over it!
> We can't go under it

> On, No!
> We've got to go through it!

SQUISH! SQUASH!
SQUISH! SQUASH!
SQUISH! SQUASH!

Refrain

Verse 2: (use blue paper or fabric for the wet pond)

Oh! Oh! A pond!
A wet, cold pond. . .

SPLASH! SPLOSH! . . .

Refrain

Verse 3: (use large wooden blocks covered with white fabric for ice floe)

Oh! Oh! An ice floe!
A creaking-cracking ice floe . . .

YIKES! YIKES! . . .

Refrain

Verse 4: (Cut out paper snow flakes or just rip pieces of white paper for snow, have a helper stand above the children to drop snow on them. Blowing it with a fan is more exciting, but harder to clean.)

Oh! Oh! A snow storm!
A whirling, swirling snow storm! . . .

HOOOO-WOOOOO! . . .

Refrain

Verse 5: (Cover a large cardboard box with a white table cloth for the den.)

Oh! Oh! A den!
A snow-covered den.

t..i..p t..o..e,
t..i..p t..o..e,
t..i..p t..o..e.

What's that?

I hear a Rumble, Grumble!
I hear a Growly, Prowly!

A POLAR BEAR! . . . ! . . . !

[Run back home, crossing each of the obstacles on the way back.]

The End.

7. *Summary:* Talk with children about their favorite part of the hunt. What parts were scary? Play a review game where you make the sound ("yikes, yikes") and children tell what part of the trip went with that sound (the ice floe).

   Optional Follow-up: Take photos or have children draw pictures of their bear hunt, and make your own classroom version of, "We're Going on a Bear Hunt."

STORYTIME STARTERS FOR PRESCHOOLERS

1. Read *The Little Old Lady Who Was Not Afraid of Anything* by Linda Williams. Children love joining in on this cumulative, action-packed tale that is especially good for Halloween time. Add the activity of making your own scarecrow to decorate the library corner. Sing or chant some Halloween or pumpkin poems.

2. Read *Little Penguin's Tale* by Audrey Wood. In this rollicking and adventurous story, Little Penguin learns why Granny's tales are important. This story is great for encouraging visual literacy. Urge children to count how many little penguins Granny has; and to keep an eye on the killer whale! Use this story to introduce a unit on the Arctic regions or on animals that live in the ice and snow. This kind of unit is good during cold or hot weather (when it takes our minds to cooler climates). Set up a nature scene, gather other books about penguins.

   Little Penguin lost some of his tale feathers as a reminder of the lesson he learned. Make a paper ice cube with the children, that will help them remember the story. Draw a picture of Little Penguin and write the story's title on one of the squares.

If you taught a poem, write that on another square. Encourage children to draw other things they remember from the story on the other squares. Have children count the sides of the squares (Can they remember how many little penguins there were? More? Less?). Give them plenty of opportunity to fold their squares and return them to their flat positions before finally taping them into an ice cube.

3. Read *Red Leaf, Yellow Leaf* by Lois Ehlert. Gather twigs, branches, and leaves to set the scene for this non-fiction book. Use poems about leaves and autumn. We like to teach children to act-out and recite the following poem. After they've learned it well, we surprise them by dropping colored paper leaves (can be obtained from school supply stores if you don't feel like cutting them out) on them during the poem. When picking them up, children can sort by color and shape.

Gently Falling Leaves

Little leaves fall gently down,
Red and yellow, orange and brown.
Whirling, whirling round and round,
Quietly without a sound,
Falling softly to the ground,
Down—and down—and down—and down.

Anonymous
(illustrated version found in the Big Book,
Sing a Song of Seasons)

4. Read *The Wolf's Chicken Stew* by Keiko Kasza. This story has a humanitarian twist, the wolf becomes charmed by Mother Hen's babies and ends up feeding them instead. It is a great way to give children some ideas about the number 100, as he bakes a 100 pound cake, gives the little critters 100 kisses, etc. Follow this story with a challenge for children to do something 100 times. How about—toe touching, hugging a favorite animal, or writing in every square on a piece of large graph paper. Do some counting rhymes or songs with this story.

5. Read *Journey Cake, Ho!* by Ruth Sawyer. This story is especially appreciated by children who know *The Gingerbread Man* well. You can lead them in thinking about how the stories are similar and different. We like to assemble toy animals for the chasing, and to bake this cake for them to chase. This is from an old family recipe, and bakes into round, fairly hard (they roll on the floor), surprisingly tasty cakes. The recipe, which

makes three rounds, is perfect for librarians and teachers. Use one for the story, eat a second with the children, and share the third for a Saturday breakfast with your own family (who probably complain that you *never* bake anything for them).

Steve's Grandmother Nooch's Aunt Clara's Old-Fashioned AP Cake

5 cups flour (use 1/2 cup cornmeal if you'd like yours to be closer to the story)
2 cups brown sugar
5 teaspoons baking powder
1/2 pound butter
1 egg
milk (She didn't say how much, remember this is Old-Fashioned.)

Beat egg in (a one-cup measuring) cup and fill with sweet milk. Combine other ingredients, mixing by hand until batter becomes stiff. Place batter in middle of three round cake pans. Bake at 350 degrees for 30 minutes or so. (Remove from oven and chase!)

---

6. Read *Rainbow Fish* by Marcus Pfister. This is basically a story about sharing and the dangers of being too proud. Children, of course, get the point but they love the sparkly fins on the illustrations and the idea of rainbows best. This storybook could be nicely connected to rhymes and songs about colors or the rainbow. Follow the reading by making sparkle collages or painting rainbows.

7. Read *Round Trip* by Ann Jonas. The black and white illustrations are indeed a round trip because, after reading about the family's day-long trip from the country to the city, we turn this incredible book upside down to read about the all-night trip back home. Each picture portrays a different scene when looked at upside down. This concept fits the cognitive world of older preschoolers who are trying to see things from other perspectives (i.e., "How do you think Billy felt when you did that?"). This is a wonderful book for looking, thinking, staring, wondering, remembering, comparing, and imagining. Children will love looking at it time and time again.

   Follow the reading by making your own upside down pictures. Have children use bold paints to make designs on large paper. When they are finished, have them label their pictures right-side-up and up-side-down. Write their words for them. Make a display of their work. Adult visitors will enjoy reading the children's labels as well.

8. Read *The Tub People* by Pam Conrad. In this story, we see a family of toy people in the bathtub suffer a great disaster: the tub child goes down the drain! He is rescued eventually, and the owner of the toys decides on a safer place to play. As you read this book, encourage children to count and recount the people, and to notice the subtle expressions on the toy people. Follow this story with an experiment in things that float and things that sink. If you have a water table available, set it up the next day with plastic people and an ivory soap bar so that children can act out parts of the story.

ACTIVITIES

1. The following book sources for songs and rhymes were used to accompany the various story themes discussed in this chapter:

Poetry

Animals on Parade and *Sing a Song of Seasons* from the Poetry Big Book series, compiled by Sara Willoughby-Herb, Steven Herb, Charlotte Klein, and James Zullinger. Elizabethtown, PA: Continental Press, 1991.

Ring A Ring O' Roses, Flint Public Library. Flint, MI: The Flint Board of Education, 1971.

Sing a Song of Popcorn: Every Child's Book of Poems, by Beatrice Schenk de Regniers and illustrated by nine Caldecott Medal artists. New York: Scholastic, 1988.

Songs

Rise up Singing: The Group-singing Song Book, by Peter Patterson & Annie Blood. Bethlehem, PA: Sing Out Corporation, 1992.

Search out your library for what you would consider three great sources for poems and songs for children: publications you would like to keep on your "professional shelf" as opposed to the children's shelf.

2. In planning for storytime, we need to choose books that can be appreciated by a group of children. Their illustrations must be large enough for all to see, the ideas clear enough to be presented without lots of explanation. Check out your library's picture book section to find other good examples of books appropriate to preschoolers in groups.

QUESTIONS

1. *What can I do about those children who have difficulty paying attention at group storytime? They distract other children, and then nobody enjoys the stories.*

   Answer: In planning for group storytime, we try to plan stories and activities that will hold most of the children's interest and attention. If you have some children who have difficulty paying attention, we suggest that you start with easy stories as listed in the "Storytime Plans for Beginning Listeners" section. This should convince them that storytime can be understandable and fun. Then, as you go on to other stories, try some of these strategies:

   - Have the child sit near you, so that you can help him pay attention better.
   - Seat the child away from events that are distracting to him such as noise from the hall, passersby, and so on. Some children need extra personal space and will get into difficulty with children who are sitting too close to them.
   - Establish clear routines that will help the easily distracted child learn to predict and anticipate what is happening. Following the same sequence of activities at storytime will help you and the child. For example, you can remind the child, "Just one more rhyme, then we have the story."
   - Try to work a lot of audience participation into your storytimes, thereby minimizing times when children's attention wanders. Read books with join-in phrases. Do rhymes and songs with actions.
   - Ask questions during the story to keep the easily distracted child thinking and involved in the story. Call on this child once or twice during each story.
   - When choosing activities, do the ones that are simple. Allow

children to explore and make decisions themselves (open-ended projects) and avoid giving several verbal directions.

- When explaining activities, speak close, make eye contact, and be sure the child looks at you, too.
- Before each storytime, speak individually and privately to the easily distracted children, telling them a little about what will be happening in order to motivate their listening. You can also prompt their attention with statements such as, "Watch for the killer whale in this story and see if he eats up Little Penguin," or "I want to make sure you are in a good place to see and hear every word of this story because something silly is going to happen!"
- Of course, during the storytime, give this child positive feedback (smile, pat, praise) for paying attention. If you told her to listen for the silly part and she is listening, look over at her knowingly. In addition, make sure that you give this child affection and praise every day. Paying attention *is* difficult for distractible children, and they need a lot of encouragement to learn how to do it. They also need lots of positive interaction with the important adults in their lives so that they don't come to think of themselves as troublemakers this early in life.

We find that a combination of these strategies works with most easily distracted children. Over time, these strategies used by calm adults will help these children learn to enjoy group time. For the few children we meet who have serious attention/distractibility problems, we have successfully used the following strategies:

- Use a volunteer (parent, teacher's aid, upper grade youngster) to act as that child's "private tutor." The tutor sits near or holds the child at storytime, quietly prompts the child's attention, and asks questions to keep the child involved in the activities. Over time, the tutor is needed less and less.
- Establish a few, clear (not strict) rules for storytime. State these rules in positive words, focusing on the alternatives to restless, distracted behavior. For example, "You have to be sitting on the rug and be quiet enough for everyone else to hear."

Establish a consequence for not following the storytime rules. We like to give all children one reminder, then follow through with the consequence on the second infraction. The consequence shouldn't be negative, just give the child an alternative to the inappropriate behavior during storytime. We have set up a table with crayons, markers, and paper or other quiet playthings; we ask the child to play at that area until the story is over. Many times we see that the child listens to the story while coloring. Perhaps having something to do with his hands actually helps the child pay attention.

2. *Is it always necessary to talk about the stories we read?*

   Answer: No, indeed! We adults don't always like to tell everyone our thoughts about books we read. Sometimes we enjoy a book, but haven't yet got our own thoughts about it into words. Sometimes we want to relish the feelings a book gives us, and not interrupt that with talking. Certainly children have such feelings, too.

   Remember, though, that the group storytime gives us a chance to direct the children's attention; talking to them in the ways suggested by language theorists and researchers. By conducting a carefully planned storytime each day we ensure that all the children in our programs have an opportunity to express and share feelings and ideas as well as the chance to interact with a knowledgeable adult around a literary event. Given this, however, it is all right if we don't always talk about stories or connect them to follow-up activities. We prefer to do this by reading additional stories rather than omitting the planned storytime. In a library, you can sometimes read another story at the end of story hour. In a preschool, read stories during transition times. In a child care setting, there are many opportunities to read to the group—as they fall asleep, during the afternoon snack, outside under a tree.

3. *How can we teach children to take care of and treasure books? When they play and do crafts at the library as they do at preschool, won't they begin to drop and step on books as some do with their toys?*

   Answer: We teach nearly everything by providing a good example. There are many things about book care that can be periodically demonstrated during storytime. For example, when you are fortunate enough to be reading a new book, show children how to open and gently smooth the pages one at a time from the front and back, working toward the middle. Let them take turns helping you. On a rainy day, take the storybook out of a plastic bag, telling the children you used that to keep the book dry. If you accidentally drop a book, pick it right up and say aloud that you don't want to hurt the book.

There are also some subtle ways to instruct children not to write on or tear books. Start the story sometimes by hugging the book, telling the children that it is one of your own, and that you keep your own books on a high shelf in your bedroom where your little two-year-old niece can't reach them. We guarantee this will spark other ideas for keeping babies and toddlers away from books. Preschoolers are specialists in the dangers of living with babies and toddlers! Preschoolers are also far more moralistic than the average adult. If you get them started on what not to do with books, they will have many more ideas than you would ever think appropriate!

Prevention is another good teacher. Make certain that books are stored in easily accessible places, you have rainy day bags available, and books don't get left on the floor after reading them.

BIBLIOGRAPHY

"Belly and Tubs" by Clyde Watson and illustrated by Wendy Watson from *Father Fox's Penny Rhymes*. New York: Crowell, 1971.

The Big Red Barn by Margaret Wise Brown and illustrated by Felicia Bond. the Big Book version. New York: Harper, 1989.

Brown Bear, Brown Bear, What Do You See? by Bill Martin Jr. and illustrated by Eric Carle. New York: Holt, 1983.

Do Like Kyla by Angela Johnson and illustrated by James E. Ransome. New York: Orchard, 1990.

The Fat Cat written and illustrated by Jack Kent. New York: Scholastic, 1971.

Fiddle-i-Fee: A Farmyard Song For the Very Young adapted and illustrated by Melissa Sweet. New York: Little, Brown, 1992.

The Gingerbread Man retold by Eric A. Kimmel and illustrated by Megan Lloyd. New York: Holiday House, 1993.

Henrietta's First Winter written and illustrated by Rob Lewis. New York: Farrar, 1990.

Journey Cake, Ho! by Ruth Sawyer and illustrated by Robert McCloskey. New York: Viking, 1953.

Jump, Frog, Jump! by Robert Kalan and illustrated by Byron Barton. New York: Greenwillow, 1981.

The Little Old Lady Who Was Not Afraid of Anything by Linda Williams and illustrated by Megan Lloyd. New York: Crowell, 1986.

Little Penguin's Tale written and illustrated by Audrey Wood. San Diego: Harcourt, 1989.

"Mice" by Rose Fyleman, in the Big Book of poetry, *Animals on Parade.* Elizabethtown, PA: Continental Press, 1991.

Mouse Paint written and illustrated by Ellen Walsh. San Diego: Harcourt, 1989.

Mr. Gumpy's Outing written and illustrated by John Burningham. New York: Holt, 1970.

Now We Can Go written and illustrated by Ann Jonas. New York: Greenwillow, 1986.

Owl Babies by Martin Waddell and illustrated by Patrick Benson. Cambridge, MA: Candlewick, 1992.

"Polar Bear" by William J. Smith, found in his book, *Laughing Times: Nonsense Poems.* New York: Delacorte, 1980.

Polar Bear, Polar Bear What Do You Hear? by Bill Martin, Jr. and illustrated by Eric Carle. New York: Holt, 1991.

Rainbow Fish written and illustrated by Marcus Pfister. New York: North-South Books, 1992.

Red Leaf, Yellow Leaf written and illustrated by Lois Ehlert. San Diego: Harcourt, 1991.

Round Trip written and illustrated by Ann Jonas. New York: Greenwillow, 1983.

Sing a Song of Popcorn: Every Child's Book of Poems compiled by Beatrice Schenk de Regniers and illustrated by nine Caldecott artists. New York: Scholastic, 1988.

The Surprise by George Shannon and illustrated by Jose Aruego and Ariane Dewey. New York: Greenwillow, 1983.

The Tub People by Pam Conrad and illustrated by Richard Egielski. New York: Harper, 1989.

The Very Hungry Caterpillar written and illustrated by Eric Carle. New York: Philomel, 1987.

The Wind Blew written and illustrated by Pat Hutchins. New York: Macmillan, 1974.

We're Going On a Bear Hunt by Michael Rosen and illustrated by Helen Oxenbury. New York: McElderry, 1989.

"Who Has Seen the Wind?" by Christina G. Rossetti and illustrated by Marcia Brown, in *Sing a Song of Popcorn: Every Child's Book of Poems,* compiled by Beatrice Schenk de Regniers. New York: Scholastic, 1988.

"Wind Song" by Lilian Moore and illustrated by Marcia Brown, in *Sing a Song of Popcorn: Every Child's Book of Poems,* compiled by Beatrice Schenk de Regniers. New York: Scholastic, 1988.

The Wolf's Chicken Stew written and illustrated by Keiko Kasza. New York: Putnam, 1987.

REFERENCES

McAfee, O.D. 1985. Circle time: Getting past 'two little pumpkins.' *Young Children.* 40 (6): 24-29.

6 READING ALOUD AND STORYTELLING

READING ALOUD

A few years ago we conducted a study with some first graders in Harrisburg, Pennsylvania (Herb, 1987). Seventy-two children were randomly selected to participate in a reading aloud experiment. Their parents, their teachers, the principals in the two schools, and even the experimenters themselves did not know the full extent of what we were measuring so as not to bias the test results. Of the 72 children, 18 were assigned to an experimental group while the remaining 54 were placed in one of three control groups. All children attended their classes as usual during the five weeks of the study. In fact, a child in the experimental group might be sitting next to a child in a control group who was sitting next to a child not even participating in the study. None of the three children was treated any differently because no one knew who was in which group.

All children received the same treat every Wednesday. A special guest (a talented children's librarian) entered the six classrooms one after the other and performed a 30 minute storytime. The order of her arrival was determined at random so that all children would eventually hear an early morning storytime one week to be followed by an end of the day storytime the next, and so on. The storytime content was planned by the librarian with the exception of one storybook. In the middle of her program, a book was inserted that had been selected by a committee of children's librarians as being an ideal read-aloud title for five- and six-year-olds. The five particular titles used in the five weeks of the study were selected at random from a larger list the committee of children's librarians had prepared. The books they selected had to be suitable for the age group, excellent for reading aloud, and available in paperback. The children's librarian was told to read the book aloud about mid-way through the 30 minute program and to read the book as it was written, attempting to keep the six readings as even as possible throughout the day.

The actual experiment began following the special story events. All children received a 10 × 12 envelope containing a paperback book from the original list prepared by the children's librarians. Some children in control groups received a book in the envelope they would be hearing at next week's story hour. Other children in control groups received books they would not be hearing in any of the five storytime. The children in the experimental group received the book they had just heard in the storytime that day, virtually minutes before. All were instructed to carry their envelopes home and show them to their parents.

Could the single reading of a book in a storytime result in any differences in children's attitudes toward reading in first grade? That was what we hoped to answer with this experiment. Children heard the storytime and took the book home on Wednesday. A note asked the parents to return the book with their child the following Monday. A small book mark in the book pocket of each book also asked if the parents had read the book to their child, how often, and who initiated the read-aloud session. Every Monday all 72 children were tested on three measures. The first was how well they could read flashcards prepared from the text of the book they had taken home. Proper nouns, nouns, verbs, adjectives, and adverbs were selected and ten flashcards were prepared and presented by a children's librarian to each child. The number of words the child answered correctly represented his or her score. A second measure was one of reading fluency. Each child was asked to read the first five sentences of the book they had taken home. The number of correct words compared to the total number read was the child's score. The third measure was a rating by the testers. The children received two numerical scores—one that measured their attitude toward the test (the sentence reading in particular) and one measuring if they read with expression. The order of testing was also varied so that children would not always receive tests before lunch or after recess, in turn getting a little bit of everything. Even the testers varied so that each child was tested by all three testers at least once in the five weeks.

That single reading of a picture storybook and the ability to take it home made a huge difference in the test results. The randomly assigned children in the experimental group were better readers of the flash cards, they read their sentences more fluently, they had a better attitude toward the reading during the testing situation, and they read with more expression. All these results were not simply a bit higher than the children in the control group, but were statistically significantly higher. We were 95 percent certain the results we had observed were due simply to allowing a child to carry home a book she had heard only one time. In sending home that book you've read to a child, you are making the child himself an ally in your plan to help the child (and the parents) love books. Whatever enthusiasm that book generated at school carried through to the home. The parents of the children in the experimental group read to their children more frequently than the parents in all the control groups.

If a single reading of a single book can have that profound an effect on children at age five or six, what will be the effects of the repeated reading of children's books on a child from birth to age five? Nothing short of a miracle. Reading aloud is the foundation of literacy. Children who learn to read early are read to. Most children who ever learn to read with ease and joy are read to. Children who love to read are read to. You can no more learn to read without being read to than a baby can learn to talk in a home without conversation. Many adults look back on their childhoods with mixed memories, but we've never heard of anyone, read of anyone, or known anyone who regrets being read to as a child. It is often part and parcel of the happiest time an adult remembers. Favorite childhood books are often friends for life—sitting on a shelf somewhere awaiting the birth of a niece or grandson. But reading aloud presents children with so much more than an enjoyable story, a funny plotline, or a tear of sympathy. It is the key to the door of the world. Books show that there are other people out there, people just like the listener, people who are also afraid of the dark or need a teddy bear to go anywhere or don't have a daddy living at home. There are also people who are not like the listener at all, who make a child wonder about the world and dream of going exploring by foot, by wheel, or by book. It is impossible to truly fathom a life without reading when one is a reader, but it is an empty, stark and often frightening reality for all the thousands of young adults who drop out of school each year. These young people not only face a life of low paying jobs or welfare, but a life stripped of allusions, perspectives, and opportunities. Lacking the skills and confidence learning makes possible, youths may turn to negative role models, because other potential role models and aspirations are absent. It is not so very hard to imagine the dismal future a child faces if the world of ideas, the world of biography, or the world of dreams is simply off limits, forever.

Literacy begins in the cradle, crawls, creeps, and pulls itself into a hesitant walk in toddlerhood, starts trotting at three and four, and breaks into at run at five. It is a step-by-step process that makes the difference between a full life and a nearly empty one.

SELECTING APPROPRIATE MATERIALS

Important attention must be paid to four parts of the reading aloud experience at once. The first is the child, the second is the book, the third is the "event," and the fourth is you, the adult reader.

1. *Know your child or children*. Developmental guidelines provide an outline for the selection of age or developmentally appropriate books to read aloud, but caregivers know best the children in their particular group, parents know best their own children. Don't be afraid to attempt to stretch children into unexplored areas and try new things. Because it is so very important to please children while reading aloud, one must repeat successes and find books like the ones your children have enjoyed. With a group of children, sample as broadly as possible so that all children hear something they find particularly rewarding. If a few children have quite simple or quite sophisticated tastes that don't match those of the majority, find time to also read-aloud to them individually at other times during the day. Watch children for signs of excitement as well as signs of boredem. Be quite attuned to your audience whether it be one or 50. We've all attended at least one talk or sermon or lecture where we wished we could change channels. Don't associate this amazingly wonderful, life transforming gift with boredom.

2. *Choose books that were created to be read aloud*. This is especially important advice when reading to groups of children. When the individual give and take of the lap experience is unavailable because of the number of children and the pictures are not large enough to be seen clearly by all, it is even more important that the chosen book delivers what it was selected to do—hold interest and produce joy. Good read alouds have language that sings with words that seem to bounce off the page and out through your mouth. The best books for the very youngest children are rhyming and rhythmic. Even as children grow older, and more sophisticated stories become appropriate, the rhythm of good books for reading aloud remains essential.

3. *The "event" of reading aloud should be a ritual in every home and every child care center in the country*. Children just love (and will fiercely protect) traditions in their lives. You will rarely forget read aloud time if you have instituted it at some regular point in an early childhood center's schedule. Should you do so, you will be reminded. Some caregivers like to put children to sleep with reading aloud as children head off for their afternoon naptime. Others like to wake their kids up with a gentle shake of a story. Still others find that reading aloud is the best way to settle children down after physical activity. Some centers have a regular storytime and a regular read-aloud time, usually taking place in different parts of the room at different times. Others find time to read aloud to their children whenever bad weather keeps the children inside or in that spare five minutes before parents come to pick up their children. In homes, it is best to find a regular time for reading aloud,

but also to always have a book ready for a wait in line, a traffic jam, or a time of sadness. Some children, especially toddlers, must do something physically while they listen. Other children are absolutely frozen in concentration, not wanting to miss a single word or glimpse of illustration. As varied as the books available for reading aloud may be, the population being read to is more so. For working parents who worry about the amount of time they are able to spend with their children, reading aloud creates some of the highest quality time available, and coupled with the ability to borrow books for free from public libraries, one of the most economically equitable. Whether it is breakfast, bedtime, bath time, or after dinner, there is a spot in your child's schedule waiting to be filled with books. Reading aloud is so important that it should never be used to threaten children, or withheld as punishment. Add minutes as a reward, but never subtract time.

4. *The adult reader must enjoy the experience for it to be maximally effective.* If you don't like the books you are reading aloud to your children you have two choices:

- pick books you do like, or
- take acting lessons.

Otherwise, your children will know you are not having the fun they are. Seriously, you want them to feel comfortable and that you are sharing something special. Sounding disinterested or as if you are going through the motions will be detected and detract from the experience for your children who are not only quite attuned to pretending (they do it too), but also worry about the happiness of their parents, often more than they let on. Read with expression, read at a speed appropriate to the pace of the story and your young listeners, and read often. Answer questions wherever you can, although sometimes questions must be curtailed when you are reading aloud to a group of children. Make certain you can always be heard by all. Audience restlessness is often caused by children unable to feel the full effects of a story because they cannot hear every word being read. And, be prepared to repeat some stories scores, hundreds, and some parents claim, more than a thousand times!

RESOURCES FOR ADULTS

The two best guides to reading aloud to children, both with preschool sections and bibliographies are:

For Reading Out Loud!: A Guide to Sharing Books with Children by Margaret Mary Kimmel & Elizabeth Segel. New York: Delacorte, 1988.

The New Read-Aloud Handbook by Jim Trelease. New York: Viking, 1989.

A SAMPLE OF READ ALOUD TITLES
FOR ONE- AND TWO-YEAR-OLDS:

The Baby's Catalogue by Janet and Allan Ahlberg. Boston: Little, Brown, 1983.

Brown Bear, Brown Bear, What Do You See? written by Bill Martin, Jr. and illustrated by Eric Carle. New York: Holt, 1983.

Catch Me & Kiss Me & Say it Again written by Clyde Watson and illustrated by Wendy Watson. New York: Collins, 1978.

The Napping House written by Audrey Wood and illustrated by Don Wood. San Diego: Harcourt, 1984.

When We Went to the Park by Shirley Hughes. New York: Lothrop, 1985.

A SAMPLE OF READ ALOUD TITLES
FOR THREE- AND FOUR-YEAR-OLDS:

Farmer Duck written by Martin Waddell and illustrated by Helen Oxenbury. Cambridge, MA: Candlewick, 1992

Geraldine's Blanket by Holly Keller. New York: Greenwillow, 1984.

Hunky Dory Ate It written by Katie Evans and illustrated by Janet Morgan Stoeke. New York: Dutton, 1992.

If You Give a Mouse a Cookie written by Laura Numeroff and illustrated by Felicia Bond. New York: Harper, 1985.

Ten, Nine, Eight by Molly Bang. New York: Greenwillow, 1983

A SAMPLE OF READ ALOUD TITLES
FOR FIVE- AND SIX-YEAR-OLDS:

Alexander and the Terrible, Horrible, No Good, Very Bad Day written by Judith Viorst and illustrated by Ray Cruz. New York: Atheneum, 1972.

Lon Po Po: A Red-Riding Hood Story from China by Ed Young. New York: Philomel, 1989.

Miss Nelson is Missing! written by Harry Allard and illustrated by James Marshall. Boston: Houghton, 1977.

Owl Moon written by Jane Yolen and illustrated by John Schoenherr. New York: Philomel, 1987.

Sylvester and the Magic Pebble by William Steig. New York: Simon & Schuster, 1969.

STORYTELLING

Storytelling is our oldest form of communication and our oldest form of entertainment. Storytelling gave us a folk tradition long before we had formed the written language to record it. Storytelling passed down remedies for curing ills that became scientifically grounded medical practice. It gave us chants to ward off evil, prayers to call for help, and a way of keeping our respective cultural heritages alive. A shared use of storytelling is one of the few things that we all have in common in this world, and at the same time, it is our personal story which makes each of us unique. Storytelling provides us with our personal history, a tale of who we are, where we came from, and a never-ending connection to our family.

The best-loved children's books tell a good story in words or pictures or both. As librarians, teachers, and caregivers, we need to demonstrate the power of stories to children in order to make them need and want that power. It is the story in the book that gives the language its magic. The story is the stitch that sews the pages together and keeps them turning in the hands of a child. Carol Bly has written an article about the six uses of story which seems particularly relevant to today's children:

1. Stories give us the experience of *other*.
   Stories often start with, "Once upon a time," which means deliberately *not now—it was at some other time.* The listener or reader must prepare to look not at what his or her eyes see—the room, the mother's or father's knee, the open window—but a kingdom which went under the ground for a hundred years, or twelve sons who turned to birds at dusk. It is not natural for your mind to be open to what is *other.* We have to cultivate this ability.
2. Stories present the *ideal case.*
3. Stories show us how to *despise evil.*
   Twentieth-century life is oddly prone to condoning evil. Yet it is more useful to recognize evil than to repress it.
4. Stories teach us *courtesy and playfulness.*
5. Stories *get us away* from our peers for a time.
6. Stories identify the *fine feelings* we have.
   The human mind recognizes a feeling only when it has words for it—which means when someone else has conversed about it (Bly, 1992, p. 2-4).

SELECTING STORIES & STYLES OF TELLING

For preschool children all styles of storytelling and types of stories should be sampled. For the younger babies and toddlers, it is probably wise to have a strong visual component to the program. Use of flannel boards, puppets, three-dimensional props, and draw talks might be more effective than the traditional "propless style." As with reading aloud, it is important for the adult to be comfortable with the material, to like what is being presented, and to enjoy the method of presentation. No matter how much some people practice, they will always feel uncomfortable using scissors when they also have to think about what they are saying. Cutting stories become dangerous in their hands! Others feel they could do anything an early childhood center may require of them, but please, don't make them talk for a puppet! There are enough choices available that teachers or caregivers should be able to select methods of presentation they particularly enjoy. Knowing what you like, what makes you laugh or cry, also helps in the decision of what stories you should select to tell. Enthusiasm for something you enjoy is contagious in a preschool crowd.

Methods of Presentation

1. *Using props and objects.* This method of storytelling is one of the simplest and often works best using the actual children's books the stories come from. It adds a nice visual touch to plop down a big stuffed Clifford, when a Clifford book is about to be read aloud. We have caught the attention of even the most exploration-minded toddlers when we pull one of our daughter's "retired" golden-haired dolls from a bag and ask the children to guess what story we are about to tell. A few guess Cinderella. A few appear to be thinking about it. Then we pull out a large stuffed bear and everyone knows and talks at once—about their bears, about their book about the three bears, about a television show they saw with Goldilocks in it. Some are still thinking and talking about Cinderella and there is always one child who begins to talk about his pet dog or cat. You have opened them up and the story has not even "officially" begun! This method is especially valuable for children who have had limited experience in groups and who have not yet learned the skill of paying attention to a book. Although technically not a storytelling method, it is important to mention the availability of "Big Books" as a kind of prop. Now that they have been around for 20 years, these large format versions of classic picturebooks are growing more popular and accessible to early childhood centers. Originally designed for group reading instruction (which is still an excellent use for them, as well), many caregivers and early child-

hood educators are using "Big Books" not to teach reading, per se, but to allow a group of young children to see the large drawings which accompany the text. They are extremely helpful to those of us over forty who are in need of bifocal lenses as well as children who need a more prominent visual image to hold their attention.

2. *Drawtalks*. Few children's books transform into a simple drawtalk story unless you happen to have illustrated the book yourself. It is easier to use a prepared drawtalk from a book of storytelling resources. These often take the shape of a story which seems to produce innocent lines until, suddenly, there is a completed object before the children's eyes. The best known is probably the "Tale of the Black Cat," where a visit to Tommy and Sally's respective houses becomes a huge cat in the final marker stroke. A very nicely presented version, with many other terrific stories, can be found in Anne Pellowski's *The Story Vine: A Source Book of Unusual and Easy-to-Tell Stories from Around the World*. Interesting variations of the drawtalk on paper are the African method of story drawing with a stick in mud or dirt, the Eskimo stories which are told by drawing in snow, and the Aboriginal (Australian) sand stories, some of which can be replicated indoors by placing the dirt or sand in a clear, rectangular baking container and placing the container on an overhead projector to project on a screen or light colored wall. In addition to samples in the book mentioned above, another excellent source is Anne Pellowski's *The Family Storytelling Handbook*.

3. *Folding & cutting stories*. Again, many of the stories suitable for these methods are found most easily in collections, but don't ever let a good idea be surpressed because it might take a little time to work out. One of the best known folded paper stories is the "The Brothers Short and the Brothers Long" which finds two sets of brothers of different heights attempting to enter two doors represented by folded paper, which eventually become a box for treasure under the skillful manipulation of the storyteller. A well-done version of this story is also described in *The Family Storytelling Handbook*. One of the best paper cutting tricks that a caregiver or teacher for preschool children could learn is the rolled paper ladder or tree, either of which serves the story Jack and the Beanstalk quite nicely as the storyteller slides out foot after foot of "vine" to the amazement of the children present. *Paper Cutting* by Eric Hawkesworth has directions to this trick that will last a lifetime.

4. *Puppets*. Puppets are probably the most powerful storytelling props available due to preschool children's willingness to sus-

pend their disbelief. Many children stare mutely at the questions of adults, especially those they don't know very well. However, it is a rare under five child who will resist the question of a puppet. We remember quite fondly a family holiday trip a decade ago when our teenage daughter began to converse with her preschool sister using a puppet in the back seat of the car. For hours, our young daughter answered questions and told the puppet stories that we had never heard her tell us or even to her confidante sister. Puppets can be purchased in many toy stores with classic folktale and fairy tale characters most readily available. It is easy enough to adapt puppets to various roles, just like actors who are playing a variety of parts. Think of the imaginary Playbill biography of our Wolf puppet.

> Wolf was last seen in the nursery school adaptation of 'Little Red Riding Hood' playing the role of the Wolf. Last season he appeared in a successful adaptation of 'The Three Pigs', a walk-on as a dog in a crowd scene in 'The Pied Piper,' and in a role he considered quite a stretch, he played the Fox in the 'Little Gingerbread Man.' He is excited about his upcoming performance as all three wolf brothers in, *The Three Little Wolves and the Big Bad Pig.*

Homemade puppets can be as simple or complex as time permits. Nancy Renfro has provided a number of guides to creating puppets that are especially suited to early childhood centers. A particularly useful guide is *Puppetry & Early Childhood Education* by Tamara Hunt and Nancy Renfro. As simple as the Renfro puppets are, it is an even simpler matter to take a paper lunch bag and draw on a face or to glue a cut-out head on a popsicle stick. It is the story and its willing audience that brings a puppet to life, not the artistic talent of the puppeteer. Elaborate sets are fun, but not required. It is not necessary to hide the fact that you are doing the talking for the puppet. Children adapt to that situation quite fast. One of the best uses of puppets in story hour settings is to make the puppet a master-of-ceremonies that introduces the next "act." Soon children will be asking for the puppet by name and cheering his arrival.

5. *Feltboard Stories.* This method of storytelling resides almost entirely in the preschool domain. The advantage of nice flannel board sets is that they last for years and can become old favorites as naturally as the story from which they came. They are easily seen on their solid dark or light background. Because of this feature they often provide a good substitute for book illustrations that

are wonderful for a small group, but cannot be seen by the large numbers of children coming to a public program or gathered together for storytime at a busy child care facility. The preparation of flannel board story pieces ranges from the hand cut and colored felt pieces that do not attempt to emulate the art in a particular book, to the more elaborate use of an opaque projector to project images from the book on to a strong, firm paper, which is then used to make a "dummy" of the characters or sets. These can then be used to make final pieces out of felt. Books that have a cumulative storyline, where things or people are added to the story one at a time, are the most easily converted to felt board sets. *The Very Hungry Caterpillar* by Eric Carle is probably the best example of the perfect flannel board story. The transformation from caterpillar to butterfly is particulary exciting in flannel board, especially if the butterfly was pre-concealed on the board before the ending. Another advantage of felt board storytelling is that the pieces serve as prompts for telling the story.

6. *Traditional Storytelling.* In their classic guide to preparing teachers, librarians, and caregivers to become storytellers, *Storytelling: Art And Technique,* the master storytellers Augusta Baker and Ellin Greene tell why the beginning storyteller would "do well to turn to folktales, stories that have been passed down through word of mouth and polished over centuries of telling. These traditional tales have the essentials of a good short story: terseness, simplicity, and vigor. They begin simply, come to the point, and end swiftly and conclusively. They are full of action, and the action is carried forward by the main characters. There are no unnecesary words, but only the right ones, to convey the beauty, the mood, the atmosphere of the tale (Baker & Greene, 1987, p. 33)." The advice we give to storytellers for preschool children would sound remarkably similar. Choose stories with simple plots, simple sequences of events, repeated and predictable language, clear characters, and topics of interest to the audience such as animals and families. Classic folktales can be found in picture book versions or in collections in public libraries. A very nice bonus of traditional storytelling is that stories come from every culture in the world as well as all cultural groups in the United States—African American, Latino, Native American, Italian American, etc. Folktales are world tales and the most natural method available for providing a multicultural environment.

7. *Family storytelling.* This special category of storytelling is a favorite among preschool audiences. It combines the elements of folk literature with a modern twist—the stories cast relatives and the teller in the starring roles. The more "story-like" the plot,

the more popular the tale will be. Young children are especially interested in tales about when they were younger than they are now (already nostalgic for when they were 2!), stories in which they play an important part in saving the day or advancing the plot, and stories in which their parents did naughty things! That is a particular favorite. Our colleague Marcia Bowers has taught classes in storytelling to unmarried teenage mothers using the "birth myths" of their own entrance into the world as a bridge to developing a storytelling relationship between the young mother and the new child. She has found this aspect of family storytelling to be particularly powerful in forging a stronger bond between mothers and children. Family storytelling can be entertaining, but behind that laughter, much truth about who we are resides. Knowledge of our personal story can be the first step to better understanding ourselves. An especially helpful resource for this type of storytelling is *A Celebration of American Family Folklore* by Zeitlin, Kotkin & Baker.

ADDITIONAL STORYTELLING RESOURCES FOR ADULTS

The Art of the Story-teller by Marie Shedlock. Toronto: Dover Publications, 1951.

Awakening the Hidden Storyteller: How to Build a Storytelling Tradition in Your Family by Robin Moore. Boston: Shambhala, 1991.

Children's Faces Looking Up: Program Building for the Storyteller by Dorothy DeWit. Chicago: American Library Association, 1979.

Juba This and Juba That compiled by Virginia Tashjian. Boston: Little, Brown, 1969.

New Handbook for Storytellers by Caroline Feller Bauer. Chicago: American Library Association, 1993.

Once Upon a Time: A Storytelling Handbook by Lucille & Bren Breneman. Chicago: Nelson-Hall, 1983.

Storyteller by Ramon Ross. Columbus, OH: Charles E. Merrill, 1972.

Storytelling Activities by Norma Livo & Sandra Reitz. Littleton, CO: Libraries Unlimited, 1987.

Storytelling with Puppets by Connie Champlin & Nancy Renfro. Chicago: American Library Association, 1985.

Tell and Draw Stories by Margaret Oldfield. Minneapolis: Creative Storytime Press, 1984.

Twenty Tellable Tales: Audience Participation Folktales for the Beginning Storyteller by Margaret MacDonald. New York: H.W. Wilson, 1986.

The Way of the Storyteller by Ruth Sawyer. New York: Viking, 1962.

A FEW COMMENTS ABOUT TELEVISION

We met some long retired public children's librarians ten years ago who told us stories about what it was like when radio programs were scheduled at the same time as their weekly preschool story-time, how worried they were, and how their programs survived. Then there was television, then video games, and soon, interactive video accessed through your home computer. No doubt about it, there is competition for the book out there in the ever-changing world. Sadly, the strongest competition for the book comes from basic physical needs not met. Young children who are alone for hours everyday have needs to be met before the benefits of reading aloud can be discussed. The child who is abused or cold, hungry or thirsty, or without shelter has primary needs which must be met before the topic of literacy can be discussed. For those children in the United Sates lucky enough to have care, food, and shelter, television can be a problem that needs to be addressed by those of us who work with young children. It is not that television is inherently bad, though much of its content is absolutely worthless, but rather that time spent in passive viewing is time not spent listening to books read and stories told. It is time most often spent in isolation from adults. In order to reduce this particularly detrimental effect of television watching we suggest the following guidelines:

1 . Encourage all adults you are able to reach to manage their children's television viewing, both content and time spent. Make suggestions for alternative habits, such as storytelling, reading aloud, and family game playing. A bibliography of "Books That Are Better Than TV" or something similar might be a helpful handout.

2. When you hear children talk of programs they have seen

and love, become familiar with them yourself, and use your familiarity with the shows and the children's interests to come up with book and story suggestions which entice children into reading.

3. When you know a good program is about to be broadcast, advertise it to your children and parents. Some children's book enthusiasts become snobbish about *not* watching television. That is not a realistic attitude in America. Use the good programs television offers to connect with your families and children. PBS still broadcasts the amazing Mr. Rogers, a hero to all preschool children and their parents and "Reading Rainbow," the wonderful children's literature-based program. The Discovery Channel broadcasts fascinating nature shows which connect nicely to children's love of animals.

4. Offer your own competition to television. The more stories you tell, the more books you read, the better the chances are that children will become lovers of books and stories and make their own decisions to limit watching. As we all know, television pales when compared to the imagination.

REFERENCES

Baker, A., and E. Greene. *Storytelling: Art and technique,* 2nd edition. New York: R.R. Bowker. 1987.

Bly, C. "The Six Uses of Story." *The Journal of the Children's Literature Council of Pennsylvania,* 6 (1), p. 2-4. 1991.

Hawkesworth, E. *Paper cutting.* London: Faber and Faber. 1976.

Herb, S.L. "The Effects of a Storyhour and Book Borrowing Strategy on Emergent Reading Behavior in First Grade Children." Doctoral Dissertation, The Pennsylvania State University. 1987.

Hunt, T., and N. Renfro. *Puppetry & early childhood education.* Austin, TX: Renfro Studios. 1981.

Pellowski, A. *The family storytelling handbook: How to use stories, anecdotes, rhymes, handkerchiefs, paper, and other objects to enrich your family traditions.* New York: Macmillan. 1987.

Pellowski, A. *The story vine: A source book of unusual and easy-to-tell stories from around the world.* New York: Macmillan. 1984.

Zeitlin, S., A. Kotkin, and H. Baker. *A celebration of American family folklore.* New York: Pantheon Books. 1982.

7 SONG AND POETRY: TAKING LITERATURE TO HEART

In our experiences with preschoolers we have met many a child for whom the first proudly "read" or memorized book was actually a poem or song. Poetry and lyrics are, for children, beautiful stepping stones toward learning how to read. But that's not what's most important about poetry and song, so we will leave this "reading" idea behind for now, and return to it only after paying rightful tribute to these literary forms. We begin this section, then, by considering the power of poetry and song and the fact that most of us know a great deal of both "by heart." This understanding of what poetry and music contribute to our own lives should be in the forefront of our minds as we think about integrating them into programs for children.

A VARIED AND MEMORABLE LITERARY FORM

When we consider the songs and poetry we know by heart, their rich variety comes to mind. Among those we remember are chants about the weather ("red skies at night . . . "), finger plays ("where is thumbkin . . . "), jump rope rhymes ("teddy bear, teddy bear . . . "), autographs and blessings ("May the hinges of our friendship never grow rusty."), and singing games ("London Bridge is falling down . . . "). We remember words to the songs we associate with important people and times of our lives (i.e., a first romance or our senior year in high school). We *even* remember some of the poems we chose to learn in English class—such as Langston Hughes' "Well, son, I'll tell you: Life for me ain't been no crystal stair . . . " or Rudyard Kipling's "If you can keep your head when all about you are losing theirs and blaming it on you . . . "

Why do we remember these? Why did we choose to practice and learn them? The poet and anthologist, Lee Bennett Hopkins, provides some answers in his discussion of the many ways poetry contributes to our lives, in his book *Pass the Poetry, Please!* He describes poetry's ability to make us laugh, present a long thought in just a few words, bring importance to ordinary events, give us a shiver, and help us appreciate and celebrate life. Quite likely these are among the reasons for our learning poetry and songs by heart.

THE PERSONAL NATURE OF POETRY AND SONG

When we offer children poems, songs, and verse, we offer them all that Lee Bennett Hopkins recounted, and more. More, because of the personal nature of poetry and song. Children make their own decisions about what poems and songs they want to "learn." Of course they don't think about learning these verses by heart in the way we adults do. However, we hear them chanting songs and rhymes as they play. And they ask us revealing questions: "Can we do that poem about the kangaroo again?" "My mom wants to know the words to that song about Miss Lucy." When it comes to songs and rhymes, children do indeed make their own decisions about what they like, why they like it, and whether or not they are going to join in and learn it. Have you ever tried to make a preschooler sing a song when she didn't want to? So we see, we are offering children opportunities to choose, learn, and use literature purely for their own, individual reasons.

UNIQUE CONTRIBUTIONS OF MUSIC

Music adds much to verse. The melodies and rhythms in songs give emphasis and shape to words and phrases, making them even easier for children to learn and remember. Music adds a structure to language in the pleasantest of ways, inviting children to join in and sing. Although we are not all singers, we can see to it that preschoolers are exposed to music through recordings and playing musical instruments.

POETRY AND SONG AND LANGUAGE DEVELOPMENT

Songs and poetry make language attractive and exciting for young children. They bring rhythm, lilt, and enunciation to everyday words. They also bring new, amazing, and fun-to-say words such as "hullabaloo!" (from Clyde Watson's poem, "Uptown, Downtown," in *Father Fox's Pennyrhymes*); and such wonderfully useful and memorable expressions as "pizza, pickle, pumpernickel" (from Dennis Lee's poem, "Three Tickles," in *Jelly Belly*). There is no doubt that good songs and poems make children want to speak, play with language, and learn new words and expressions.

Poetry and song also teach children powerful lessons about learning. Children learn that words and ideas can be made to stick in our minds by the addition of rhythm, repetition, and the clustering of thoughts. Many young children chant instructions to themselves as they go about their first errands, while helping with the shopping, for example, "Bread, bread, a loaf of bread!"

Certainly it is the rhythm, rhyme, and predictability of songs and poetry that make them good subjects for children's first attempts at reading the words in a book. There are many ways we can use songs and poetry to expose preschoolers to beginning reading skills and concepts. We can post large charts displaying a picture and words to a favorite verse. We can also obtain Big Books of songs and rhymes, so that children can see the big print of the words and letters as they chant the rhymes. We can make children individual copies of a poem they know well, so that they can take it home to "read" to someone. We can help children make up new verses to songs that have predictable word patterns (e.g., "The Wheels on the Bus" or "The Farmer in the Dell"). Writing these new verses gives children an opportunity to watch us print their own words in large letters right before their eyes. They typically pay great attention to these kinds of writing. And they learn about how to make letters and what kinds of sounds the various letters make while they are watching. Children who have many and repeated opportunities to look at the words to songs and rhymes they love to chant will be advantaged children when it comes to more formal lessons in learning how to read.

We proceed now to some ideas for sharing songs and poetry with young children. This section is divided into two developmental periods, infancy and toddlerhood, and the preschool years. We end each section with a short list of additional resources for this kind of literature.

USING SONGS AND RHYMES WITH INFANTS AND TODDLERS

1. Integrate songs and rhymes into baby's routines. Many poetry and Mother Goose books for these youngest children include rhymes about daily life. If you work at a child care center, meet

with other staff persons to decide on some songs and rhymes to use with the children at particular routine times. Print them on colorful posters and hang up in appropriate places (changing table, sink, etc.) to remind caregivers to use them regularly with the children. After a few months you might want to introduce some new ones, though don't forget to review children's favorites.

- One of our favorite collections for this purpose is *Catch Me & Kiss Me & Say It Again* by Clyde & Wendy Watson. In this small volume, which will catch the young child's eye as well as ear, you will find rhymes about waking up, dressing, tooth-brushing, fingernail snipping, chasing, and going to bed — all with language that will dance off your lips and call you to play! Memorize just a few of these to chant along with daily routines, and see how poetry brightens everyday activities.

2. Teach baby some games based on songs or rhymes. Use these regularly at play time.

- *Trot, Trot to Boston* compiled by Carol F. Ra is a great source of play rhymes. Each rhyme is accompanied by clear instructions regarding actions (knee-bouncing, tickling), and also includes some ideas about how your baby might react to and participate in the rhyme.
- Jane Yolen's *The Lap-Time Song and Play Book* is similarly helpful in its presentation of nursery songs.

3. Review the songs and rhymes you know by heart and think about learning some more. Those of us who work with young children should have a host of songs and rhymes that we know by heart, and can recite, as they say "at the drop of a hat." Make certain that your repertoire of songs and rhymes includes some from each of the categories below:

- *Lullabies and night songs.* Singing our babies to sleep at nap and night-time is one of the gentlest things we do for them. A restful rocking and singing with a baby who is nodding-off is often one of the most relaxing things we caregivers do for ourselves as well. *I See the Moon: Good-Night Poems and Lullabies* is a nice source for these.
- *Rhymes and songs that have a "surprise" ending.* For example, some jig-jogging rhymes ("This is the way the ladies ride") end with us gently toppling baby off the foot. Some

finger creeping rhymes ("Round and round the garden") end with a tickle. Pause just before you get to this surprise event, to help baby notice that something important is coming. When babies play these rhymes time and time again, they learn to anticipate the surprise ending. When this happens, they are learning to remember routines and trust their ability to predict events—important first learning events. You will know when this learning has begun, as babies often get squirmy and giggly just before the surprise.

- *Songs and rhymes that help baby learn about his body.* Face tapping ("Brow bender"), foot patting ("Shoe a little horse"), and toe counting ("This little pig") all help baby sense the separateness of parts of his body, as well as providing interesting sensory experiences.

4. When using play rhymes and songs, adapt the actions to individual baby's preferences. Some babies prefer softer or harder tickling and tapping. Some babies prefer a warm hug as a surprise ending, rather than a spilling or a trip up into the air. Some babies just don't like to be tickled at all, so touch them more firmly and substitute a squeeze for any major tickles recommended in the instructions. Adapt your vocal play as well, remembering some babies are charmed by gentle voices, others only by raucous recitations.

5. In general, use a special voice when reciting songs and rhymes to these youngest children. Emphasize the pattern of the rhyme, exaggerate and dramatize some of the words, and make your face and voice expressive. Speak and sing slowly enough for baby to follow the words.

6. Respect baby's wishes for repeated performances. Take the word, "Again!" as a compliment, and do and redo. The baby who says "more" or "again," is actually telling you much more—that he really likes that rhyme, that he wants to learn/remember it, that he knows a word that can make wonderful things happen, and that he thinks you are someone he can count on to listen to what he says. So, how *can* you say no?

7. Keep alert to baby joining in with you on words, melody, or action. This shows that the baby is learning, remembering, and enjoying your literary play. Occasionally hold back and let baby do the actions, words, and so on. Show him your enthusiasm for his learning.

8. Allow baby to learn rhythms such as rocking, clapping, and bouncing by just watching you. Don't try to force baby to make "Patty-cake" by taking his hands in yours. Allow him the oppor-

tunity to join in when he is able to internalize the rhythm. Then the rhythm and expression will have come from the baby, thereby creating another opportunity for him to develop competence.

9. Fill-in baby's name in verses whenever possible. For example, in "Patty-Cake" say "put it in the oven for Sylvie and me." In Clyde Watson's "Phoebe in a Rosebush" (*Catch Me and Kiss Me and Say It Again*) and "Nanny Banny Bumblebee" (*Father Fox's Pennyrhymes*), one can easily substitute baby's name. We like chanting these rhymes with a knee-bounce, ending them with a hug—making each one a love song for baby. Even four- and five-year-olds who have been bounced to these request them "again!"

10. Many books of songs and rhymes for the youngest children are really designed for adult use. Make sure that toddlers, themselves, have books of songs or rhymes in their homes or child care centers. These should be child-sized and have child appeal. In addition to enjoying the books themselves, they can carry the book to an adult asking the adult to "read" it.

SONG AND RHYME BOOKS FOR INFANTS AND TODDLERS

Resource Books for Caregivers

Jane Yolen's Mother Goose Songbook selected by Jane Yolen and illustrated by Rosekrans Hoffman. Honesdale, PA: Boyds Mills, 1992.

Lap-Time Song and Play Book edited by Jane Yolen and illustrated by Margot Tomes. San Diego: Harcourt, 1989.

Michael Foreman's Mother Goose selected and illustrated by Michael Foreman. San Diego: Harcourt, 1991.

Ring-a-round-a-rosy: Nursery Rhymes, Action Rhymes and Lullabies compiled and illustrated by Priscilla Lamont. Boston: Little, Brown, 1990.

Trot, Trot To Boston written by Carol F. Ra and illustrated by Catherine Stock. New York: Lothrop, 1987.

Wendy Watson's Mother Goose selected and illustrated by Wendy Watson. New York: Lothrop, 1989.

Verses Related To Children's Daily Routines

Catch Me & Kiss Me & Say It Again written by Clyde Watson and illustrated by Wendy Watson. New York: Collins, 1978.

A Cup of Starshine selected by Jill Bennett and illustrated by Graham Percy. San Diego: Harcourt, 1991.

Rhymes Around the Day illustrated by Jan Ormerod. New York: Lothrop, 1983.

Picture Books for Toddlers Containing a Single Verse

Fiddle-i-fee: A Farmyard Song for the Very Young. Adapted and illustrated by Melissa Sweet. Boston: Little, Brown, 1992.

The Itsy Bitsy Spider retold and illustrated by Iza Trapani. New York: Whispering Coyote, 1993.

Old MacDonald Had a Farm retold and illustrated by Carol Jones. Boston: Houghton, 1989.

Cardboard Series for Toddlers to Carry About

Clap Hands, All Fall Down, Say Goodnight, Tickle, Tickle written and illustrated by Helen Oxenbury. New York: Macmillan, 1987.

I'm a Little Teapot, Knock At The Door, Pat-a-cake, Pat-a-cake, Round and Round the Garden illustrated by Moira Kemp. New York: Lodestar, 1992.

USING SONGS AND RHYMES WITH PRESCHOOLERS

As with infants and toddlers, we try to use song and poetry in spontaneous ways, sprinkling them throughout the day. However, we use them in more formal ways, as well. For example we teach children verses to help them celebrate seasons, we teach songs related to our units of study, we may teach songs or poems composed by particular writers, and we may encourage children to "compose" their own verses.

INFORMAL USES OF POETRY AND SONG

One of the ways we share songs and poetry with children is to see to it that children have an opportunity to hear them and to hear someone else enjoy them, and to observe the various purposes of this kind of literature as described by Lee Bennett Hopkins. In this case, we are not really attempting to teach the songs or rhymes to the children, just to give them opportunities to listen, enjoy, and/or learn them. Let's consider how we can informally sprinkle verse into the daily lives of preschoolers:

1. Find some walking and marching rhymes (we like "Hup, Two, Three, Four, Marching Out the Castle Door" from *Catch Me and Kiss Me and Say It Again*), to chant while children are walking along in groups.

2. Find some songs and rhymes that go with various kinds of large motor play—jumping, swinging, rocking, see-sawing.

3. Find some songs and rhymes that can be acted out (as opposed to finger rhymes), to use for rainy days.

4. Learn some finger plays that you and the children can use for those few times when children have to stand or sit and wait. Acting out finger plays can keep children interested and active while waiting in their jackets for a late bus, waiting for a guest storyteller, and so on.

5. Make a collection of weather verses ("It's Raining, It's Pouring") to use on days when the weather really is worth remarking about.

6. Gather some rhymes (perhaps jig-jogging ones, ones that would incorporate the child's name) which you could chant while holding a child on your lap. Teach these to children early in the preschool year, using them as a way to give each child special attention. You will find them requesting these rhymes later on, when they need some lap time.

7. Make certain that your listening center contains recordings of poetry and songs. If possible, find books that accompany these songs and rhymes. Children would enjoy a recording of their classmates singing or chanting the verses.

8. Make certain that your classroom library always has poem and song books in its collection. These are the most memorable of books, and they inspire children to "read" to themselves as well as to one another during free-choice time.

FORMAL USE OF POETRY AND SONG IN THE PRESCHOOL

This refers to deliberately planned activities, where we choose to teach children particular verses and we focus on them as developmental experiences. Below are some suggestions for integrating poetry into your developmental programming for preschoolers:

1. Make poetry and song a regular part of one of your group storytimes. This is especially important for children who are hesitant to talk. Many children find this group language activity the safest, easiest way to participate in activities requiring speaking.
2. Teach poems and songs with topics that relate to units you are teaching.
3. Use poems and songs as activity starters, relating them to a wide variety of developmental learning (See fig. 7-1).

Developmental Activities this Poem Could Inspire—

- *Movement Activity*—Act out the poem by making a circle on the rug to represent the pan, have children be the sausages, exiting the "pan" at appropriate times.
- *Music Activity*—Have children choose or improvise rhythm instruments that make sounds similar to POP and BANG, to use at appropriate times in the rhyme. This rhyme can also be sung to the tune of "Twinkle, Twinkle Little Star."

FIG. 7-1 Using the Poem, "Ten Fat Sausages' as an Activity Starter

Ten Fat Sausages

Ten fat sausages sizzling in the pan,
Ten fat sausages sizzling in the pan,
One went POP and another went BANG.
There were eight fat sausages sizzling in the pan.

Eight fat sausages sizzling in the pan,
Eight fat sausages sizzling in the pan,
One went POP and another went BANG.
There were six fat sausages sizzling in the pan.

Six fat sausages. . . .

Four fat sausages. . . .

Two fat sausages sizzling in the pan,
Two fat sausages sizzling in the pan,
One went POP and another want BANG.
There were no fat sausages sizzling in the pan.

Anonymous

- *Language Arts/Prereading*—Print the poem on chart paper, reading it with the children, sometimes drawing your finger under the words as children read it with you. Let them find the big words, POP and BANG on the chart, and draw circles around them. If that is successful, they might like to find the long word, sausage, too.
- *Early Number Concepts*—This poem has some number concepts that preschoolers won't quite understand. If you act it out with them or illustrate it with felt pieces, however, it gives them an early experience with grouping by twos and an experience with subtraction as counting backwards. They will understand that at the end of each stanza there will be fewer and fewer sausages. They will also understand the concept of two.
- *Personal-Social Development*—Talk about and taste some other noisy foods, such as popcorn, rice crispies, crackers. Do the children like noisy foods?

4. Make home-made books of songs and poems that your children know. Children will enjoy taking these home to share with their families.
5. Occasionally connect an illustration or art project to a song or poem. This gives children the opportunity to consider what the poem might mean to them and to represent the same idea in a non-verbal manner.
6. Print your children's favorite poems on large notecards, attach a picture, and store them in a poetry file that children can use. Occasionally have them choose the "Poem of the Day" from this collection of favorites.
7. Include poem books, song books, and poetry collections on your center's bookshelves.
8. Make certain that the poems and songs you choose represent the diversity of your children, as well as the diversity of our nation, its peoples, and its languages. You will find that this variety will allow every child to find a kind of verse that is right for him or her.
9. Accompany songs and rhymes with body movements that express rhythm, and with body movements that express the events in the verse. This makes for a very active experience with the literature, and makes it much easier for children to learn.
10. Select some stories-in-rhyme for your children's bookshelves. These stories are easy ones for children to learn to memorize.

POETRY AND MUSIC RESOURCES FOR PRESCHOOL SETTINGS

RESOURCES FOR ADULTS

Children' Counting-out Rhymes, Finger plays, Jump-rope and Bounce-ball Chants and Other Rhythms written by Gloria T. Delamar. Jefferson, NC: McFarland, 1983.

Go In and Out the Window: An Illustrated Songbook for Young People edited by Dan Fox. New York: Holt, 1987.

Make a Joyful Sound: Poems for Children by African-American Poets edited by Deborah Siler. New York: Checkerboard Press, 1991.

Rise Up Singing edited by Peter Blood-Patterson and Annie Blood-Patterson. Bethlehem, PA: Sing Out, 1992.

Stretch, Jiggle, Jump; Sing a Song of Seasons; Feasting and Fun, Animals on Parade, a Poetry Big Book Series compiled by Sara Willoughby-Herb, Steven Herb, Charlotte Klein, and James Zullinger. Elizabethtown, PA: Continental Press, 1991.

POETRY COLLECTIONS FOR CHILDREN

It's Halloween written by Jack Prelutsky and illustrated by Marylin Hafner. New York: Greenwillow, 1977.

Play Rhymes selected and illustrated by Marc Brown. New York: Dutton, 1987.

Read-aloud Rhymes for the Very Young selected by Jack Prelutsky and illustrated by Marc Brown. New York: Knopf, 1986.

Surprises selected by Lee Bennett Hopkins and illustrated by Megan Lloyd. New York: Harper, 1984.

Talking Like the Rain: A Read-to-Me Book of Poems selected by X.J. Kennedy and Dorothy M. Kennedy and illustrated by Jane Dyer. Boston: Little Brown, 1992.

SONG COLLECTIONS FOR CHILDREN

"Wee Sing Series," *Wee Sing, Wee Sing and Play, Wee Sing Silly Songs* selected by Pamela C. Beall and Susan H. Nipp. Los Angeles: Price, Stern, Sloan, 1982.

POEM/STORY BOOKS FOR CHILDREN

Brown Bear, Brown Bear, What Do You See? written by Bill Martin, Jr. and illustrated by Eric Carle. New York: Holt, 1983.

Each Peach Pear Plum written and illustrated by Janet Ahlberg and Allan Ahlberg. New York: Viking, 1979.

Mama Don't Allow written and illustrated by Thacher Hurd. New York: Harper, 1984.

Mommy, Buy Me a China Doll adapted by Harve Zemach and illustrated by Margot Zemach. New York: Farrar, 1966.

SONG/PICTURE BOOKS FOR CHILDREN

Hush, Little Baby adapted and illustrated by Margot Zemach. New York: Dutton, 1976.

The Lady With the Alligator Purse illustrated by Nadine B. Westcott. Boston: Little, Brown, 1988.

London Bridge Is Falling Down! illustrated by Peter Spier. New York: Doubleday, 1967.

Oh, A'Hunting We Will Go written by John Langstaff and illustrated by Nancy Winslow Parker. New York: Atheneum, 1974.

Ten In the Bed illustrated by Penny Dale. Pleasant, CA: Discovery Toys, 1988.

The Wheels On the Bus illustrated by Paul O. Zelinsky. New York: Dutton, 1990.

ACTIVITIES

1. Go browsing through the children's poetry and music sections in your local public library, looking for verses you would like to share with children. Look for these in the non-fiction sections.

2. Obtain some of the song and poetry collections from the resource lists in this chapter. Choose a poem or song you would like to use for each of these routine times:

- wake-up
- nap time
- clean-up
- rocking
- dressing

QUESTIONS

1. *How difficult is it to find songs and poetry that reflect America's diversity?*

   Answer: This is getting easier as many publishers, appreciating the needs of their customers, are putting out special multicultural catalogs and promotional publications. However, these publishers won't necessarily have many examples of song and poetry books, and all of them may not be appropriate for preschoolers. You will also need to browse through edited volumes of song and rhyme in order to find examples of diversity yourself. *The Horn Book Guide To Children's and Young Adult Books* which reviews every children's book published each year is a valuable resource for your search as well, especially because of its subject index. See Appendix A for additional selections of materials representing all of America's cultures.

2. *We agree that preschoolers often pretend to read songs and poems, but that isn't really reading, is it? Isn't that just memorizing?*

   Answer: Memorizing a story or a rhyme *is* a first step toward reading. It is the beginning of reading. After children can do this, they will begin to match the words they have memorized to the words printed in the book (especially if an adult occasionally points this out to them). It is important for us to acknowledge the importance of these first "memorized" books, to show enthusiasm for the child's accomplishment, and to refer to it as "reading." Unfortunately some children's efforts are met by a demoralizing, "You can't read. You just memorized that!" We must inform important people in these young reader's lives that this kind of reaction discourages children. Teach them to encourage and build on these first attempts to remember the words.

RESOURCES

Pass the Poetry, Please! written by Lee Bennett Hopkins. New York: Harper, 1987.

BIBLIOGRAPHY

"Uptown, Downtown," written by Clyde Watson and illustrated by Wendy Watson from *Father Fox's Pennyrhymes*. New York: Crowell, 1971.

I See the Moon: Good-night Poems and Lullabies selected and illustrated by Marcus Pfister. New York: North-South Books, 1991.

"Three Tickles," written by Dennis Lee and illustrated by Juan Wijngaard from *Jelly Belly*. New York: Bedrick Blackie, 1985.

The Lap-Time Song and Play Book edited by Jane Yolen and illustrated by Margot Tomes. San Diego: Harcourt, 1989.

8 INTEGRATING LITERATURE EXPERIENCES INTO EVERYDAY ACTIVITIES

Current theory and practice in early childhood education emphasizes the importance of children's learning experiences being integrated. With children's literature, we think of integrated learning as occurring when:

1. Children are read to at various times of the day—not just at storytime or bedtime.
2. Books and stories are incorporated into the various themes that we study with children (seasons, the family, etc.).
3. Books and stories play a part in children's learning about non-literary topics, such as mathematics, science, history, and human understanding.
4. Adults encourage children toward reading-related play.
5. Children develop their own personal literary preferences: favorite books, authors and illustrators, favorite times and places for reading.

Children seem to learn best, to remember best, when their learning experiences are integrated in these ways. They learn that literature is important throughout their lives and not just at a certain place or time of day. In this chapter we will offer some suggestions for carrying out these integrated literature experiences.

VARY TIMES AND PLACES FOR READING

Remember that the first way we teach is by showing, so model being a reader yourself. Let children see the many ways that you use reading and let them see variety in your reading. Keep a bulletin board or pocket for important notes. Talk out loud as you write or post the note, letting children hear that the written message is important to you. Keep reference books (dictionary, encyclopedia, phone book) handy, and periodically use them when children can notice. We have found that preschoolers enjoy using encyclopedias, perhaps because they are so heavy and important looking. We often mark a page that interests children (e.g., whales) by placing a bookmark with a picture drawn at the top and placed in the appropriate page. Every now and then, share with the children something that you read from a newspaper, magazine, or book. Let them see some of your reading materials.

To be certain that children read at various times and places, try some of these ideas:

In preschool centers,

- allow children to take books to other appropriate areas of the classroom. For example, let them go to the housekeeping area, the waiting room of the "doctor's office," or the art tables where they may be used to inspire writing or drawing.
- read or recite poems to children at unexpected times. For example, read during a snack, on the bus, under a tree at recess, or while they are painting.
- allow children to check out classroom books so they can share these familiar stories with someone at home.
- invite guests (grandparents, siblings, etc.) to come to school and sit in the library corner to read to children during play time.
- write a very simple note to parents (for example: "Show and Tell is tomorrow," or "Bring a shoe box to school, please"). Print the words in large letters, add a simple drawing to help children remember the words. Then teach the children how to "read" the note, before sending it home with them. They will no doubt enjoy showing off their reading ability.

In libraries,

- have guest-readers for special occasions, stationing them around the children's room on special "reader chairs," so that children can take books to them to be read aloud.
- schedule some story hours that involve special times of day (for example, bedtime ones where children can wear pajamas) or special places (for example, tree stories under the library's "back yard" tree).

- offer a special story time in conjunction with important community events or attractions like a science or art museum, or the fair grounds. Make certain the storytime area is conducive to listening, free from other distractions, and the children will truly enjoy the story break.
- share the idea of varied times and places for reading in your outreach work, in parent meetings, and with daycare providers.
- if you provide books for child care centers or preschools, suggest that teachers borrow some cardboard books for the children to use when they pretend to read to their "babies" in the housekeeping center.

In homes,

- consider having books in every room of the house—bathroom books, bedroom bookshelf, coffee table books, or cookbooks in the kitchen (preschoolers enjoy browsing in colorful cookbooks while a parent cooks nearby).
- use book reading time to help your child learn to soothe herself. For example, read stories together when children are fearful of stormy weather, read lots of stories when children are not feeling well, or read stories when children are over stimulated and need help in settling down.
- take turns reading stories, that is suggest that your child "read" to you. Encourage the child to tell you a well-known story while turning pages of the book. This kind of pretend reading is a good step toward reading.
- point out familiar logos and public print to your child so that she can learn to read those signs. For example, children can find restaurant and store signs, bathroom signs, and labels on cereal boxes.

INCORPORATE BOOKS AND STORIES INTO THEMES

In preschool settings we typically use thematic units for organizing our planning for the children's experiences. These themes are usually broad in scope, and can incorporate all kinds of activities.

Some popular preschool themes include fall, winter, spring, summer, animals, plants, food, our community, and our family. We suggest that each time you choose a theme, go to the library to look for related literature. Try to find a variety of related literature, that is, non-fiction books, books with stories, poems, songs, maybe even a story for telling. To find all of these you will have to look both in the fiction and non-fiction sections of the library. Ask if your library has a subscription to *The Horn Book Guide To Children's And Young Adult Books.* The index is useful in identifying children's books published each year that are related to topics of interest to children and their caregivers (e.g., dogs, the senses, friends).

When you choose these books for themes, be certain that you only choose books which are good, quality literature. It is better to have fewer books than to force children to hear or see ones that are not well written or illustrated. Similarly, avoid books that are merely written to teach a lesson. Children quickly see these intentions to manipulate their thoughts and are turned off by the reading.

Consider making some homemade books with the children; books that are related to the activities you did during the unit of study. Homemade books can be sewn together, stapled, laced, or bound using a book binding tool. The books' contents can be written by the adult using words the children suggest, illustrated or "written" by the children, and can include songs or poems learned or photographs.

Some homemade books we have made with children are:

- *Babies,* written during a unit on "Myself." This contained photocopied photographs of the children when they were babies. The children provided the words to accompany the pictures. Examples include, "Babies like to suck on their thumbs and fingers a lot," and "You have to keep babies in cribs or baskets. Be careful of dogs."
- *Our Little Book of Experiments* written during a unit on "Water," and based on some of the children's water "experiments." The children drew pictures of their experiments and dictated sentences to the teacher: "I put blue playdough and red crinkly paper and water in a jar. I stirred it. It is sticky. It turned purplish-red." or "I made it out of paint. In a few days it got dried up. Now, I'm going to make a new one next year."
- *When We Grow Up* written during a unit on "People at Work." For this book, each child drew a picture of him/herself at a future job; and dictated sentences for the teacher

to write: "I want to be a daddy who drives a truck and takes care of a baby." or "I want to be a school bus driver, and I will take kids to school and then take them back home again."

These homemade books are very popular with families, so we like to put a library card and pocket in the back to allow children to take turns taking them home to share with their families.

STORYBOOK LINKS WITH NON-LITERARY TOPICS

The first way we can do this is to provide children with books that cover a wide range of topics. Literature, specifically story, can have a powerful influence on our ability to understand concepts related to other disciplines, such as science, mathematics, human understanding, and history. Story often brings an explanation or order to our everyday experiences. Consider for example how the story of "The Little Red Hen" is a good explanation and reminder for most of us, as to why we all should pitch in and help when there is work to be done. For our young children, as well, story often provides a metaphor for understanding concepts about life. For example a story about the life of a tree can give children a memorable explanation and a sense of the importance of preserving forests. We need to be aware of good, age-appropriate storybooks that might provide this type of understanding for children. Some examples are:

- *Antarctica,* motivating children to think about preserving nature.
- *A Chair for My Mother,* portraying a family who successfully weather a disaster and save together for an important purchase.
- *Giving,* portraying the ups and downs of giving, with the ups winning.
- *Henrietta's First Winter,* stimulating empathy for animals' hibernation chores.
- *Owl Babies,* reassuring children who miss their mothers that waiting will be rewarded.
- *The Rainbow Fish,* demonstrating that giving is better than receiving.

A second way we can do this is to help children be aware of the content in stories that is related to topics such as mathematics or history. We do this by periodically pointing out this kind of information as we read. In many of the finest storybooks, content related to number, human emotions, places, and situations is present in subtle ways. The author and illustrator are not preachy or instructional. The lesson is available through interactions among the child-listener, the book itself, and the adult-reader. The following guidelines suggest ways to interact with children around books. These can be used individually and with children in groups.

1. *Before Reading*—Tell the child the title, and look at the cover illustration together, hypothesizing what the story might be about: "I wonder what will happen in this story?" or "Look at their eyes; I wonder what they are thinking about." If children have any experiences related to the story, let them tell about them now. This will help them connect to the story and they won't feel as much need to interrupt during the story. End this discussion by giving children something to listen for during the reading: "Maybe you are right. Let's listen and see if these owls really are afraid."

2. *During the Story*—Periodically ask questions to see if children understand the story events. Add words and point out aspects of the illustrations where you feel explanations are necessary. For example, you might have to help a child understand what a fish's scale is. When the author uses a word you suspect the child does not know, briefly define the word as you read. Ask thinking questions regularly to keep the children involved. If possible, ask questions about what might happen next. Give children plenty of time to look at the pictures, touch them, and talk about them. The story told by the pictures is as important as that told by the words. Respond to children's comments about the story; though in group situations balance this with the goal of keeping the whole group involved. Encourage children to join in during appropriate parts of the story (e.g., where words or phrases are repeated). Encourage them to use new words and concepts from the story.

3. *After the Story*—Connect the story's events with predictions made before and during the story. When possible relate the story to aspects of the children's lives. Let children ask questions and comment on the story. In a pre-

school setting, show children where you will put the book so they can find it to look at again later.

ENCOURAGE LITERACY-RELATED PLAY

Child developmentalists consider play to be one of the most important learning experiences in young children's lives. Play provides opportunities for children to practice new skills, experiment with new ideas and understandings, and generally enjoy processes rather than products. We suggest four ways to incorporate literacy into children's play, thus enriching their play as well as encouraging their enjoyment of literacy.

HELP CHILDREN CREATE THEMATIC PLAY

We have learned that children's play is stimulated and expanded when it revolves around themes and purposes. We see thematic play when children set up a pretend grocery store, doctor's office, or beauty parlor. We can teach children subtle lessons about the importance of reading and writing by incorporating literacy-related props in their thematic play. Remember that at the beginning, children need adults joining their play; interacting in ways that encourage (but not force) them to use the literacy props. Some examples of these props and of adult encouragement follow.

1. *Doctor's Office props*—prescription pads, pens, scales, thermometer, Snellen chart, books, and magazines for waiting room. *Adult encouragement*—"Do you want me to write down her temperature, doctor?"; "That's OK; I'll read my baby a storybook while we wait our turn."
2. *Grocery Store props*—bags with store name, cash register, pencils, paper, play money with denomination number written on it, prices written under foods, and pre-written shopping lists so shoppers can check off what they want to buy. *Adult encouragement*—"Why don't I help by being the banker who makes the money; come to my counter to tell me how much money you need for your shopping."; "Should I help you make some store signs—OPEN, CLOSED, SALE TODAY?"
3. *Post Office props*—Stamps, envelopes, paper, scale, cash register, pens, markers, stickers, old greeting cards, labeled

boxes for receiving mail (Shippensburg, Air Mail, Barcoded, etc.), various posters, and signs. *Adult encouragement*—"I wish I could send my mother a birthday card; is there anything I could use?"; "How much will it cost to send a letter all the way to France? Do I need a special stamp?"

4. *Restaurant props*—Store sign, telling whether serving breakfast, lunch or dinner, chalk board listing the day's specials, pencils and note pads for wait-staff, cash register, play money, and menus. *Adult encouragement*—prepare some real food which the children could order (peanut butter sandwiches, cheese sandwiches); write the words in large print on the menu so that children can easily point to and read the food they want.

5. *Dog Kennel*—This one was suggested by children after two classroom visits by interesting dogs; it came to be one of the adults' favorites. The props included cardboard boxes for the child-dogs, name tags for the "dogs" to wear and for their kennels, numbers for over the kennel doors, empty food bags, bowls, telephone, leashes, cash register, play money, and a dog-training book. A favorite part of this play for the adults was an idea the children came up with where the adults were to take the "dogs" out for walks where they practiced obeying various commands such as "Stay," "Sit," etc. A teacher's never had such a sense of control!

ACT OUT STORIES TOGETHER

Many children's stories lend themselves to acting out, using puppets, costumes, or props. Children enjoy remembering events and language from the stories in their enactments. The mere act of taking on another role teaches young children a great lesson in considering another's perspective. Among the stories that lend themselves to being acted out by preschoolers are folktales such as *The Gingerbread Man, Chicken Little, The Three Bears, The Three Little Pigs,* and *Red Riding Hood.* Try other favorite stories as well though.

ENCOURAGE CHILDREN TO ACT OUT STORIES WITH MINIATURE TOYS

Many books contain ideas for dramatic play with small toys. And what a pleasant change from the kind of toy play pushed on children by Saturday morning television shows! Line up some play people before reading children Pam Conrad's *The Tub People* and its sequel *The Tub Grandfather*. After the story, discuss acting out these stories about toy people being lost and found. Children will have other ideas based on their own experiences with losing toy people. Laura Newton's *William the Vehicle King* and Virginia Lee Burton's *Mike Mulligan & His Steam Shovel* and *Katy & the Big Snow* are great stories for suggesting incorporating creative dramatics into vehicle play.

Don't forget to link stuffed animals to stories. When reading stories about bears, rabbits, and other animals, relate them to the stuffed animals you have in your classroom.

ENCOURAGE CHILDREN'S PLAYING-AT-READING

Finally, playing with literature should also include children playing at reading themselves. It is through pretending to read, practicing the various phrases and expressions of "book-talk," and reciting memorized passages while turning pages that children begin their first excursions into the world of reading. These experiences are always enjoyable for children because they have the same properties as other play—children choose to do it themselves, they make up their own rules, and they can experiment with the reading without fear of being right or wrong. This pretend reading builds a foundation of reading experiences that will only help children when they begin to read in more formal ways in the primary grades.

We can encourage playing-at-reading by providing good storybooks that are easily memorized by children and interesting enough to children that they want to repeat them time and time again. Some titles we have found successful for this purpose are:

- *Brown Bear, Brown Bear, What Do You See?*
- *I Went Walking*
- *The Little Old Lady Who Was Not Afraid of Anything*
- *The Very Hungry Caterpillar*

Be certain to introduce these books with enthusiasm. Read them as often as requested by the children and make them available for the children to play-read with.

We must remember not to correct children who are playing at reading, just as we would not correct children who are playing store. For example we don't insist that children playing store get all the prices marked correctly or behave exactly as the storekeeper does. If we were to do this children would become preoccupied with correctness, have less fun, and probably not choose to play it as much. When children play at reading, they need this same ability to experiment, be creative, and feel free.

DEVELOP PERSONAL PREFERENCES

One of our most important goals in integrating literacy experiences revolves around each child developing a personal relationship with literature. We hope each child will have favorite books, favorite authors and illustrators, favorite parts of stories, favorite lines of text, and so on. The best way to achieve this is to model it yourself. Introduce a book at storytime saying, "This is one of my favorite stories" or "Last year's nursery class just loved this story. It really made them laugh."

In addition to modeling our own personal preferences, we can be alert for children's developing favorites. Hold a show and tell in which children bring their favorite books to storytime, showing their favorite picture in that book. Let children have turns picking out stories to be read aloud. If you have a book-buying budget, save some of that money to use during the year for children's choices. When you borrow library books, you will find children becoming attached to some of them. Use your reserved money to buy permanent copies of some of these books.

ACTIVITIES

1. Using the *Horn Book Guide* and your local public library's catalogue, develop a bibliography of good children's books to use with one of these thematic teaching units (or one of your choice): Forest Animals, Making Friends, Animals that Work for Us, Machines, or Farms. Include fiction, non-fiction, poetry, and song in your bibliography.

2. Plan a creative dramatic center that focuses on one of these play themes: housekeeping, library, veterinarian, ballet, or other theater. Describe the literacy-related props you would use. Tell what kinds of play routines you would encourage with the children. Locate some children's books related to those themes.

QUESTIONS

1. *Isn't integrated learning a problem for children who have learning disabilities? I've been told that direct teaching is most successful for these children since they often have problems with*

paying attention, organizing their behaviors, and transferring their learning to other situations.

Answer: First, although these are frequently cited characteristics of children with learning disabilities, there are many children who do not exhibit these behaviors. Therefore, we can't make such predictions about these children. Secondly, the integrated literacy activities we've suggested are similar to many of the teaching strategies recommended for children with learning disabilities: active learning, use of concrete examples, opportunities to learn how to get along with others, letting children choose, and carry out their own goals. As for children who have difficulty sticking to task, managing their own behaviors, and following goals, the teacher who sees her role as a supporter of children's learning and play (as we've suggested) will be able to monitor and encourage children who have these kinds of learning difficulties. When the teacher is actively observing and joining children's play, the play has more focus and will foster more purposeful behaviors even in children who have problems with attention.

2. *Should we encourage preschool children to write, too? Is pretend writing similar to pretend reading?*

Answer: Yes and Yes. Both pretend reading and writing involve children's playful experiments with printed language. You might find some children who play at writing before they play at reading, and vice versa. Both should be treated respectfully. Most of the play themes suggested contain opportunities for children to play at writing, for example, addressing envelopes at the post office, drawing numbers and faces on play money they make, or writing prescriptions. Remember to praise children's efforts, and not insist that their play writing be accurate (in letter form, arrangement, or spelling), so as not to punish their efforts and interest.

Teachers can model writing for children by doing it in front of them on regular occasions. Some ideas for teachers' writing are—making lists, writing thank you notes, keeping a daily record of something such as the weather, and writing names of children who wish to be next to play in a center.

Sometimes we find that children's books provide incentives for children to try out writing. For example, children enjoy making their own alphabet and counting books by writing the letter or number and adding illustrations by cutting and pasting magazine pictures.

Children like to make their own books. The first books they make usually begin with a picture, not a story. The words come after the pictures. In such cases we see books that say, "This is a boat. This is my mother. This is red." In their first books, children are usually most preoccupied by assembling something that looks like a book. They love cutting paper and stapling the pages together, cutting and pasting pictures inside, and putting their names on it. It will take a bit of adult support to encourage children to put writing on the pages inside. Over time, however, scribble-writing will appear, perhaps printing of a familiar letter or two, requests for an adult to write a word under a picture. Older preschoolers like to copy words and may even begin to write some themselves. Finally, words such as "This is . . . ," "Once upon a time . . . ," and "The end" will begin to appear more in children's homemade books.

BIBLIOGRAPHY

Antarctica written and illustrated by Helen Cowcher. New York: Farrar, 1990.

Brown Bear, Brown Bear, What Do You See? by Bill Martin Jr. and illustrated by Eric Carle. New York: Holt, 1967.

A Chair for My Mother written and illustrated by Vera B. Williams. New York: Greenwillow, 1982.

Giving written and illustrated by Shirley Hughes. Cambridge, MA: Candlewick, 1993.

Henrietta's First Winter written and illustrated by Rob Lewis. New York: Farrar, 1990.

I Went Walking by Sue Williams and illustrated by Julie Vivas. San Diego: Harcourt, 1990.

Katy & the Big Snow written and illustrated by Virginia Lee Burton. Boston: Houghton, 1973.

The Little Old Lady Who Was Not Afraid of Anything written by Linda Williams and illustrated by Megan Lloyd. New York: Crowell, 1986.

Mike Mulligan & His Steam Shovel written and illustrated by Virginia Lee Burton. Houghton, 1939.

Owl Babies by Martin Waddell and illustrated by Patrick Benson. Cambridge, MA: Candlewick, 1992.

The Rainbow Fish written and illustrated by Marcus Pfister. New York: North-South, 1992.

The Tub People by Pam Conrad and illustrated by Richard Egielski. New York: Harper, 1989.

The Tub Grandfather by Pam Conrad and illustrated by Richard Egielski. New York: Harper, 1993.

The Very Hungry Caterpillar written and illustrated by Eric Carle. New York: Collins, 1987.

William the Vehicle King written by Laura Newton and illustrated by Jacqueline Rogers. New York: Bradbury, 1987.

9 CONNECTING WITH FAMILIES TO SUPPORT LITERACY IN THE HOME

The link between family efforts and children's learning is so firm-ly established that family involvement is considered a necessary component of high quality, early childhood programs across the United States. Successful family efforts include a range of activi-ties, from family members spending time in their child's pre-school or library, to learning specific techniques for fostering their child's development. And definitions of family range from children's par-ents, to foster families, grandparents, older siblings, baby-sitters, caregivers, and so on. Because the nature of our family programs should be as diverse as the families and their situations, this chap-ter considers a variety of ways we can reach out to families.

TECHNIQUES FOR REACHING OUT TO PARENTS

Although most of the chapter deals with ways we can share our knowledge of books and other materials to support emerging liter-acy with families, we need to consider family outreach as a two-way street with the traffic of learning going in both directions. That is, we have much to learn from children's families. For example, parents are typically much more skilled in interpreting their young children's language than the professionals who work with their chil-dren. Parents can help us understand children's unique ways of pronouncing words and expressing their wants and needs. Parents can share the knowledge of their children's personality characteris-tics and interests. When we know this kind of information, we can respond to children more effectively and plan programs that will meet children's needs more easily. Finally, when we show parents our interest in learning from them they feel more open to learning from us.

WORKSHOPS AND PARENT GROUP MEETINGS

The group meeting is one of the more common methods for sharing information with children's families. These are usually held in the libraries or child care centers where the children are enrolled. This is desirable since it gives parents an opportunity to share their children's experiences there. In planning group meetings, consider these factors:

- What day and time is most convenient for families?
- Will families need transportation or child care assistance?
- How can you make this a positive experience for the families who attend so they will want to return in the future?

When outlining the content of the meeting itself, try to keep its length to one or one-and-one-half hours, and don't present more than three kinds of information so that families won't feel overwhelmed. You will be successful if you think of the meeting as if it were a short party. Be certain to greet everyone, show them around the facility, and introduce families to one another. Think of the content you present as a buffet (your "guests" will pick and choose from the array), provide handouts or other take-homes to remind them of the messages presented, thank the families for coming, and make at least tentative arrangements for another get-together. Some suggestions for group meeting topics are:

1. Any of the topics presented in the first several chapters of this book, for example, reading to children or conversation techniques. Plan to present the information by demonstrating the techniques for the families, then allowing time for them to do guided role-play.
2. Topics related to important transitions in children's lives. Have a program for expectant parents that introduces them to first literature such as Mother Goose and play rhymes. Have programs about how to share literature as well as which are appropriate books for toddlers, who are so often "on the go." Parents of preschoolers are often very interested in what they can do to lay a foundation for learning to read and write.
3. Topics that can help families with the routines of parenting. Many parents would appreciate a workshop on "Rainy Day Activities" that would include—homemade recipes for playdough, glue, and paint; arts and crafts for preschoolers; choosing developmentally appropriate toys; making toys from household scraps.

4. Present workshops that can help families with the more difficult aspects of parenting such as toilet-training, beginning child-care, and disciplining. You might bring in experts to present some of these subjects, but allow time for parents to consider and practice how they might implement the techniques in their own situations. Remember to include advice about how to integrate language into all these kinds of learning. Model the use of clear, consistent, and positive language which will guide both children and parents through difficult times. Provide book and other resources for parents to check out.

WORKING WITH INTACT GROUPS

In some cases we are fortunate enough to work with one group of parents over a year or more. This often happens in child care and preschool programs. This gives us an opportunity to plan programs across the year, programs which parallel children's learning in the center. Certainly these families would profit from the kinds of workshops described earlier. We can then personalize their group meetings, link them to their children's classroom program, and extend them even further with topics such as those we suggest below.

1. Involve the families in making materials for children's learning in the preschool program. For example, sew homemade, blank books for the children to use for drawing and writing. At the next meeting, bring back the books with their children's work inside. Explain and point out examples of children's emergent writing and drawing skills which are closely related to emerging reading skills.

   Other examples of materials parents can help make: pattern pieces for puppet making (you can accompany this with information on the importance of imaginative play); assembling a classroom art kit for each child (accompanied by information on the importance of early experiences with these activities); labels to be placed on shelves so that children know where to return toys; songs or stories on tape for children to play at the listening center or at home.

2. In cases where all participating family members can read, provide an article to be read before the group meeting so that they can discuss its content at the meeting, applying it to their own particular situations. We began to do this based on a parent's request and found that families appreciated the opportunity to think ahead about the meeting topic and save the articles for future use.

3. Have a family storytelling meeting. Share information on the importance of storytelling. Suggest some topics that families might tell about. The book, *A Celebration of American Family Folklore* is a wonderful resource for this and provides samples for idea starters. Two favorite storytelling topics with our parent groups were, "When I was a Preschooler Like You" and "My Favorite Relative" (again, from childhood). We had markers and crayons available so that parents could illustrate these stories. Then we had them write the stories or tell them on tape. Children loved having these!

COMMUNICATE REGULARLY WITH FAMILIES

Whether we have parent group meetings or not, we should try to share observations with families regularly, at least weekly. One way to do this is with weekly newsletters, but we can't be certain that all families take time to read them or that all children manage to deliver them. We have found that the most important link between the home and the program is the child. So the ideas we recommend here all have one thing in common: they enlist the child as an important courier of the information and link between home and learning agencies.

1. Send home crafts or other projects that children have worked on, and will enjoy telling about. Sometimes attach a short, pre-printed note to parents (e.g., "We read *The Very Hungry Caterpillar* and made these beautiful butterflies!"), to give parents information about how the project is related to children's literature experiences.

2. Send home projects that encourage interaction between the children and their families. For example, have the children draw pictures of their favorite tub toys on already cut-out bathtubs. Attach this pre-printed note to families: "We read *The Tub People* today, and made these pictures of our own bathtub toys. Can you guess which toys these are?" Or, after reading Pat Hutchins' *Changes, Changes* send children home with a set of paper geometric shapes, and tell them to bring the completed picture back to school or library for sharing with others.

3. If you make monthly calendars, or booklets to record activities that the children do in the program, let the children take turns taking these home to share with families. If possible put photographs in the booklets. Children will

enjoy reading these with their families and talking about their learning activities.

4. When possible send home words to favorite songs and rhymes. Parents are often charmed by the verses preschool children repeat at home, but can't quite figure out the words. They appreciate a copy of the "original"—the more to enjoy their child's creative touches!

INVITE FAMILIES TO PARTICIPATE IN PROGRAMS FOR CHILDREN

In many library programs, such as storytimes for infants or toddlers, parents or caregivers do accompany the children. This provides a rich opportunity for parent education. Even in cases where parents are not usually with children, such as at child care or nursery, it is good to hold a special family storytime periodically so that parents can come and participate. These are perfect times to demonstrate strategies for reading to children and talking to caregivers about their reading. Some ideas for strategies to model follow.

1. Demonstrate how imaginative playthings can be made from materials around the home. For example, follow up a story about animal or people homes with a craft activity where children make a home from an appropriately cut paper bag and some crayons. Make a boat from a milk carton cut in half. Make people from toilet paper rolls. Make musical shakers from yogurt containers.

2. As you read to the children, remember to demonstrate your patience with them, your ability to be expressive, your ability to ask questions that keep children involved and listening, and your enjoyment of the story along with the children.

3. Consider choosing books that will interest parents as well. Stories about children's lives with their families are good examples of these. The presence of a mischievous child in a story always attracts parents' attention. Sometimes an author's ability to sympathize with both parent and child, while solving the problem, is a good lesson for all. Shirley Hughes and Jan Ormerod are fine examples of such authors.

We need to remember that parents often ask very serious questions at informal times, for example after a meeting. Often these are the times they first tell us of a worry about their child. Or they ask our opinion about their child's development. These are questions they have been concerned about but perhaps hesitant to call and set up a meeting. It seems easier to slip in these questions at less structured or formal times. This is one reason we should always take time to chat with families, to be available for socializing before and after programs. For these occasions, we always have to be prepared with names of resource persons or agencies, booklets, or whatever else might help us provide some support and direction for those families.

SPECIAL CONSIDERTION FOR THE BLOOMING READER

Each spring and summer librarians and teachers are asked, "My child seems almost ready to read; what should I do to help?" The parents asking this question do want some help, yet their situation indicates that for some time they have been providing a splendid environment for the nurturing of reading. Just because the child seems "about to read" doesn't mean that the parents should now exchange their old habits for teaching. In fact, if you've ever spoken to a child who was an early reader (who read before going to school) about how he or she learned to read, you find the *absence* of a teacher stands out in the explanation: "Nobody taught me. I just learned it."; "I just figured it out."; "I always knew how to read!"; "How do kids learn to read? That's easy; you read to them!" The pride and self-assuredness with which these children answer inquiries about how they learned to read is a reminder that when we teach children in a structured and deliberate way we often prevent them from that feeling of having learned it themselves. This notion of children acquiring reading skills as opposed to *being taught* those skills ought to be part of the response to parents' inquiries about their children's reading. Emphasize reading together, taking turns in question-asking and explanation, and plenty of before and after reading discussions of meaning, character, place, and plot.

There is a body of research that supports the notion that children can acquire reading skills without being directly taught to read. Children who acquire reading skills through daily encounters with literacy in their home environments usually have parents who might better be described as reading partners than reading teachers. Margaret Clark (1976) and Dolores Durkin (1966) attempted to identify specific aspects of the home environments of young children who learned to read themselves. They found that the homes of these children were rich in reading and writing materials. In addition, they found that the children's parents had certain characteristics in common: they read and *reread* to their children, they valued reading themselves, they fostered their children's reading as together they encountered natural occasions for reading (reading labels on food containers, road signs, store signs), and they took time to answer children's questions and to talk about their experiences. Again, we see an absence of direct teaching: no reading workbooks, stacks of word cards, or testing children on letter and word recognition.

What does a parent do, then, instead of teaching the child to read? How can teachers and librarians help parents be effective reading partners for children whose reading is about to bloom? By tuning-in to the children, we will find some answers. These children often ask, "Help me find a book that I can read." They ask for help in spelling words and "sounding" out words; they ask parents to read certain books over and over again. Such behaviors tell us that they are ready to try reading a book if it seems easy enough and has an easily remembered text that someone is willing to read until learned. Furthermore, they know enough about letters and their specific shapes that we can go ahead and point out letters (even some words) in those familiar books, and they might remember them!

As caregivers, teachers, and librarians, we can help by assisting children and their parents to locate those books that are just right for the child who is learning to read. We can also suggest some specific supportive, but *not* didactic, kinds of interactions that help children make discoveries about reading. We have provided a selection of parent-child activities that may help children's reading bloom and several books that are helpful for parents who want to be partners in the blossoming of their children into readers.

ACTIVITIES FOR PARENTS AND CHILDREN

Some of the activities which follow can be natural extensions of reading aloud sessions. Others seem to be separate activities. In either case, be certain to introduce them in an atmosphere of normal parent-child interactions, allowing lots of input, direction, and inspiration to come from the child.

1. *Read Together.* While reading books, parents can:

   - periodically trace under words with finger while reading,
   - point out an often repeated word,
   - drop their voice to allow the child to supply a word or phrase when suspecting that child may know it (since you've read the book so many times) and
   - praise the child's ability to read along and supply missing words with statements such as, "Wow, you're getting to be a real reader!"

2. *Read to Dolls.* Encourage your child towards imaginative play that could include reading to someone—dolls, dogs, etc. Playing school and playing house are good times to introduce reading. If you still have some cardboard books from the child's infancy and toddlerhood, retrieve them right away. They are great first readers as they often have only one or a few words per page. Even if they appear "baby-like," your child will accept them within a play context.

3. *Label Storage Areas.* Read the Berenstein's *The Messy Room,* if your child needs motivation to tidy up the living quarters. Let your child help decide the words to use for labeling containers and shelves. Then, with daily practice in cleaning the room, these labels will become easily recognized words. Be sure to print the labels in large, bright, simple printing. Don't capitalize the letters. Most print encountered in books is actually in the lower-case form.

4. *Keep a Message Board.* Record simple family messages each day on a slate that your child can easily see. Print the message (again, using lower-case print where appropriate) when your child is with you, sounding out words as you print. Encourage your child to remind other family members to read the message board. Short but meaningful messages are best: "Bill, call your mother"; "Baseball game—6:00"; "Buy food."

5. *Read Public Print.* When on walking and driving trips, share your goals with your child. Let your child know that you are looking for a sign that says "Locust Lane" or "H & R Block." Your child will enjoy helping you find it.

6. *Encourage Child to Read to You.* When your child has memorized a book (song, story, poem, etc.), ask if she would "read" it to you. Be very accepting as your child

will probably make some errors. Praise these readings with enthusiasm. Polish will come over time.

RESOURCES FOR PARENTS

Cushla and Her Books by Dorothy Butler. Boston: Horn Book, 1980.

This is a true story about the first years in the life of Cushla, a severely handicapped child. The author chronicles the importance of children's books in Cushla's life and their positive influence on her language and cognitive development. In doing so, she discusses in detail Cushla's favorite books and her reactions to them. This heart-warming and motivating story is an inspiration to others who are parents or teachers of young, handicapped children.

Learning to Read by Margaret Meek. London: The Bodley Head, 1982.

A very useful and motivating volume, this book was written for parents who aspire to be partners in their children's reading development. Meek provides information on all stages in the process of learning to read, from preschool to the teenage years. Characteristics of children's learning, reading interests, useful child-adult interactions, and book lists are given for five major developmental stages. This useful guide will see parents through many of their children's school years.

Reading Begins at Home by Dorothy Butler & Marie Clay. Exeter, NH: Heinemann Books, 1981.

This book is a short, easily-read introduction to techniques parents can use to encourage their children's learning to read. The techniques revolve around naturally occurring family activities (e.g., reading library books together or writing birthday thank-you notes). Parents will find the suggestions practical and immediately useful.

THE READING FATHER

The purpose of this section is to bring together some things we know about children and books with some things we know about fathers. The proposed book selections and activities are based on the notion that we can bring them together best by considering the roles fathers *typically* play in the development of their young children.

The positive contributions of fathers to their children's learning has only recently made a noticeable entry into the professional literature in child rearing. It is no wonder that what we read about fathers in the popular press is frequently critical. How often we read about fathers who spend little or no time with their children, who abandon families, who refuse to pay child support, who abuse their wives and children. It must be difficult for good fathers and for young and aspiring fathers to read so much of this.

In fact, a father told us this during a parent meeting at Shippensburg University's nursery school. We had just read the picture book, *Piggybook,* by Anthony Browne (New York: Knopf, 1986). Mothers and fathers in the audience laughed and exchanged knowing glances during this story about a father and sons who learn how very much Mrs. Piggot did for them. They learn the lesson only *after* she suddenly leaves home, and they slip into a "piggy" existence. A good-natured father, still smiling from the story, asked if there weren't some books for his children that portrayed fathers in a kinder light.

That father's question was the catalyst for this focus, which had been emerging for some time based on our own observations and experiences in the world of two-working-parent families. More and more fathers are escorting their children to storytimes (especially evening programs), handling bath and storytime at home, and helping to rear their children. For those of us who have such husbands, we know what a treasure they can be. For those of us who are promoting children's books and reading, shouldn't we consider whether our services are responsive to this new and growing clientele—reading fathers? Do we appreciate and respond to the traditionally differential roles of mothers and fathers in the lives of children? Since so many of our culture's children's book promoters are women, isn't it possible that some biases toward mothers' roles in children's lives influence our choices of books to read and promote? In fact, don't women just love Anthony Browne's *Piggybook?*

FATHERING AND CHILDREN'S DEVELOPMENT

Because the unique and positive aspects of fathering are new to child development's professional literature, there are few commonly accepted descriptors of the roles fathers play in development. More and more information is coming, however. For the purposes of this section we have chosen to explore three aspects of fathering. These are relevant to the task of bringing together fathers, children, and books. They are also based on research data on fathering. These three aspects can provide guidance for those of us who are searching for good children's books that portray fathers positively and that fathers especially enjoy reading to their children.

Father's Indirect Role

Several studies examining the importance of fathers in their children's development cite the indirect but significant nature of their influence (Silber, 1989). That is, support by the father is associated with greater parenting competence in mothers. Marital harmony, as well as agreement between parents, facilitates children's competence in social and academic areas. Selections of children's books that portray fathers in these supportive roles provide models that competent fathers appreciate and with which they can easily identify. They also can provide models of competence for less knowledgeable or young and aspiring fathers. The four following books all portray fathers in a supportive role; all are available in paperback.

And I'm Never Coming Back, by Jacqueline Dumas (Toronto: Annick Press, 1986). In this amusing, "slice-of-life" story, the father does indeed play a supportive role. His role appears more in the pictures than in the text. It is obvious that the whole family has had a bad day, and that father and mother are each tending to the cares of one of their two daughters. If the father had not been at home to take care of Jennifer, Louise and her mother couldn't have run away from home. The last picture of the story tells us how important the father's support was in the plan to restore individual peace and family harmony.

Daddy Makes the Best Spaghetti, by Anna Grossnickle Hines (New York: Clarion, 1986). A sweet and funny book, this one gets its charm from the Daddy's personality. He's really quite a guy: picks up his son at day care, does the grocery shopping, cooks, and plays jokes to the amusement of his family. The story and pictures portray a loving and realistic picture of a working family.

Owl Moon, by Jane Yolen and illustrated by John Schoenherr (New York: Philomel, 1987). This Caldecott Award winner is an outstanding book for many reasons, one of which is the portrayal of a father whose hobby, owling, adds a unique and quietly beautiful experience to his daughter's life and to the imagination of this book's readers.

Sunshine, by Jan Ormerod (New York: Lothrop, 1981). This delightful wordless book and its companion volume, *Moonlight,* tell of the beginning and end of a day in the lives of a competent young girl and her busy, sometimes disorganized parents. It is so easy for parents to identify with this couple, that no one is surprised to read on the back flap that these stories are based on Jan Ormerod's own family. The father pictured here is certainly supportive of the mother as he wakes to his daughter's kiss and prepares breakfast for her and Mommy who is still in bed. As he reads with his daughter, Mommy gets a few more ZZZZZ's.

Father's Playful Role

One child development text discusses this topic under the heading, "Fathers and Other Playmates." The authors (Scarr, Weinberg & Levine, 1986) acknowledge that babies become attached to their fathers as readily as to their mothers, but that fathers are not just good mother substitutes. They provide distinct kinds of play experiences for their young children. Researchers find that fathers differ from mothers in that they engage in more physical play, and invent new and unusual games (Yogman, et al. 1977). Father's interactions with infants indicate they devote a larger proportion of that time to play than do mothers. In their play with fathers, infants show higher states of excitement and more complete withdrawals of excitement than in play with their mothers—higher and lower emotionality.

Perhaps it is a bit of a leap to apply these data to a discussion of choosing books for fathers and children, yet much early reading is playful in nature—finding pictured objects, making animal noises, remembering words. In preparing this section, we interviewed some fathers and a male first-grade teacher concerning what kinds of books they especially enjoy reading to children. We will quote the first grade teacher because his statements included concepts brought up by the others interviewed. He began by cautioning, "I'm afraid this will sound sex-stereotyped to you!" He went on to say, "I like action-packed books, ones with dialogue so I can change voices, ones with discrepancies and illustrations that require that you think. I like reading the kids stories that are really goofy and silly. But I also like reading ones that play on the kids emotions, stories that make them sad." Do these descriptors sound familiar? We were startled by the parallels to research on fathers playing with their infants—physical play, unusual and inventive play, and emotional highs and lows.

Do children appreciate these aspects of playing with fathers? In one research study with toddlers, two out of three children chose to play with their fathers when given a choice (Clarke-Stewart, 1978). A student of the first grade teacher we interviewed told his babysitter, "I don't know why, but I feel like I want to own every book Mr. Z reads us in school."

Certainly there are lots of fine children's books containing the elements of good stories listed previously: Mitsumaso Anno's interesting picture books, Chris Van Allsburg's intriguing, mysterious stories and pictures, Jack Prelutsky's and Shel Silverstein's funny, playful poetry, Robert Munsch's crazy tales. We've chosen two stories for storytime presentation that should interest fathers for their storylines as well as their portrayals of fathers as important characters.

Abiyoyo, by Pete Seeger and illustrated by Michael Hays (New York: Macmillan, 1986). This book tells the tale of a little boy and his father who gain control over a terrible giant through their wit, magic, and music. The story begs to be enacted, as Pete Seeger has so often done—to be sung, danced to, faces made, voices dramatized. And the inside note from the author on the value of storytelling is touching. It motivates the reader to tell the story creatively.

Bea and Mr. Jones, by Amy Schwartz (New York: Bradbury Press, 1982). This is a wonderfully funny story about a kindergartner and her father who are tired of their days at school and work, respectively. The pictures and words are full of discrepancies which keep reader and listeners giggling—Bea sitting at conference table dressed in her father's business suit, Bea's father being a whiz at the colored lollipop game played in kindergarten as he answers, "Vermilion red, I believe."

Sensitivity to the Traditional Role of the Father in the Family

Researchers observing mothers and fathers while their four- and five-year-olds were at play, noted that fathers were more likely than mothers to interfere with what has been traditionally labeled sex-inappropriate play and to reward sex-appropriate play (Langlois & Downs, 1980). Fathers are more actively and personally concerned that their children engage in appropriate sex-role behaviors. Sometimes this strong concern on the part of fathers becomes a difficult family situation when the father is placed in a non-traditional role. It can be difficult for the children and mother, as well as the father. For example, some unemployed fathers, who see their family responsibility in the role of "breadwinner" will feel a loss of status in the family. Unemployed fathers report feelings of stress and disruption (Cobb & Kasl, 1977), of depression, anxiety, and lack of sleep (Moen, et al., 1981).

The new roles that fathers are playing in their families' lives may be somewhat threatening to what males learn about sex-role expectancies. Two kinds of children's books are responsive to this aspect of fathering—those that portray fathers playing both traditional and loving roles in families, and those portraying strong males managing less traditional roles, such as caregiving for children and other aspects of home-making.

Dad's Back, Messy Baby, Reading, Sleeping, by Jan Ormerod (New York: Lothrop, 1985). This series of books for toddlers stars a creeping baby and her/his dad. The dad is a playmate, but is also obviously a caregiver. He shows admirable patience in his interaction with his child who reminds us of the expression, "terrible twos." His periodic frowns and tired face tell the reader that he can be annoyed, yet he treats his baby with loving consistency. In *Messy Baby,* the reader watches Dad pick up toys, books, and food from the floor of Baby's room while Baby is crawling behind him undoing all. Dad finally turns around, looks exasperated, then recovers and hugs the baby saying, "Never mind. Let's start again!"

My Dad Takes Care of Me, by Patricia Quinlan (Toronto: Annick Press, 1987). This story is told in the voice of a young boy, Luke, whose unemployed father takes care of him while his mother works. Although the boy worries about telling his friends that his dad, not his mom, takes care of him, he realizes there are lots of things he likes about this arrangement. He and his dad play together, talk together, cook together, and love each other. At the story's end, they also do homework together because his dad is taking a course by mail. In a great picture that combats a popular stereotype of females, Mom helps both Luke and his dad with their math homework!

Tight Times, by Barbara Shook Hazen and illustrated by Trina Schart Hyman (New York: Viking, 1979). The action in this book logically precedes that of *My Dad Takes Care of Me.* It tells of the immediate stress a whole family experienced when the father lost his job. This is another story with emotional highs and lows. It depicts a family coping in a loving way during a very difficult time, and a father who remains sensitive to his son's needs at a time when he is clearly feeling crushed, himself. This story touches the thoughts and feelings of readers in ways that are good for us all.

Up North in Winter, by Deborah Hartley (New York: Dutton, 1986). This is a story of days of old when people, not just men, were bold. We imagine this story taking place out on the Great Plains, and the author tells us it is in the year

1911. The family was nearly running out of food, the father was commuting a great distance to find work. The father missed his train home one cold and icy night; the start of an exciting adventure that engages young listeners and portrays a brave and loving father.

Using Fathering-Related Books in Programs

We can apply this information on fathering to make our program offerings more suitable to the interest of fathers and to provide children with experiences related to their needs for fathering. A few idea starters follow.

1. Teachers and librarians might check content of their story-times and lending libraries for stories related to these aspects of fathering. Such stories should enhance fathers' enjoyment in reading to their children.

2. Teachers and librarians can assess and, perhaps, revive their own use of the playful and emotion-laden stories that fathers seem to enjoy. This seems especially important for children who do not have lots of contact with fathers. A good resource for these kinds of stories is Jim Trelease's *The New Read-Aloud Handbook* (New York: Penguin, 1989). In fact, those of us who have heard Jim Trelease in person or on tape recognize elements in his reading aloud that are related to research on fathering—physical play, humor, emotionality.

3. Book displays in libraries could be constructed with greater attention to portraying positive father models. Librarians working with programs serving at-risk populations might consider the subtle caregiving lessons portrayed in many of the books reviewed here. Might these books be used to provide important lessons for teenage fathers or new fathers whose best fatherhood potential has yet to emerge?

4. How about a child care center or public library Fathers' Day Program that celebrates literary fathers. Children could vote for their favorite book-fathers. Fathers could vote for their favorite book-children. Fathers who are writers, illustrators, or storytellers would be great as guest speakers. Displays of books that star fathers would be a fine background against which librarians could present their father patrons with "I'm a Reading Father!" awards or badges.

ACTIVITIES

1. Make a list of resource agencies and persons in your community whose services might be of interest to the families you serve. Gather brochures when available.
2. Plan a networking program for the families you serve, where you invite members from other community agencies to set up tables and share information. For example, invite persons representing community child care facilities.

QUESTION

1. *What can we do to get more families to participate in parent education programs?*

   Answer: In cases where participation is low, we need to consider why families don't participate and try to tailor the program to their needs. For example, child care or transportation might be problems. A volunteer group might help with this through funding or participation. Also consider the unique parenting needs of your population and try to provide programs that meet their needs. Families have to deal with varied concerns such as helping language development of bilingual children, dealing with developmental problems like learning disabilities or attention-deficit disorder, and single parenthood. Find out which are the concerns in your community and focus on some of those topics at your group meetings.

   Another solution is to take your program to the families. For example many high schools have programs for teen parents. Consider getting involved in these programs, teaching young parents how to read, and talk with their children. Make a connection with the local Well-Baby Clinic and other medical facilities to offer instruction and materials.

RESOURCES

A Celebration of American Family Folklore by Steven Zeitlin, Amy Kotkin, & Holly Baker. New York: Pantheon, 1982.

The New Read-Aloud Handbook by Jim Trelease. New York: Viking, 1989.

BIBLIOGRAPHY

Changes, Changes written and illustrated by Pat Hutchins. New York: Macmillan, 1987.

The Berenstein Bears and the Messy Room written and illustrated by Stan and Jan Berenstein. New York: Random House, 1983.

Piggybook written and illustrated by Anthony Browne. New York: Knopf, 1986.

The Tub People written by Pam Conrad and illustrated by Richard Egielski. New York: Harper, 1989.

The Very Hungry Caterpillar written and illustrated by Eric Carle. New York: Philomel, 1983

REFERENCES

Clark, M. 1976. *Young fluent readers*. London: Heinemann.

Clarke-Stewart, K.A. 1978. *And daddy makes three: The father's impact on mother and young children*. Child Development, 49, p. 466-478.

Cobb, S., & Kasl, S. 1977. *Termination: The consequences of job loss*. Department of Health, Education and Welfare Publications No. 77-224. Washington, D.C.: U.S. Government Printing Office.

Durkin, D. 1966. *Children who read early*. New York: Teachers College Press.

Langlois, J.H., & Downs, A.C. 1980. *Mothers, fathers and peers as socialization agents of sex-typed play behaviors in young children*. Child Development, 51, p. 1237-1247.

Moen, P., Kain, E., & Elder, G. 1981. *Economic conditions and family life*. Washington, D.C.: National Academy of Sciences, Committee on Child Development and Public Policy.

Scarr, S., Weinberg, R.A., & Levine, A. 1986. *Understanding development*. New York: Harcourt Brace Jovanovich.

Silber, S. 1989. "Family influences on early development." *Topics in Early Childhood Special Education,* 8(4), p. 1-23.

Yogman, M.W., Doxin, S., Tronick, E., Als, H., Adamson, L., Lester, B., & Brazelton, T.B. 1977. "The goals and structure of face-to-face interaction between infants and fathers." Paper presented to the biannual meeting of the Society for Research in Child Development, New Orleans.

APPENDIX A
CHILDREN'S BOOKS

In this appendix we have listed selected titles from 1993 and 1994, figuring that the longer the title has been around, the better the chance caregivers, teachers, and librarians have seen it or heard about it. Along with a half-dozen reissues, most of these titles are new.

ABC & LETTER BOOKS

Bernhard, Durga. *Alphabeasts: A Hide and Seek Alphabet Book.* New York: Holiday House, 1993.

A gamelike alphabet book where animals are concealed in beautifully painted, natural settings.

Eichenberg, Fritz. *Ape in a Cape.* San Diego: Harcourt, 1952.

This re-released alphabet book is a classic for its playfulness.

Hatay, Nona. *Charlie's ABC.* New York: Hyperion, 1993.

A clever use of photographs in which the featured word has color in an otherwise black & white photo.

Howland, Naomi. *ABC Drive!* New York: Clarion, 1994.

An ABC for motorized vehicle fans.

Mackinnon, Debbie. *My First ABC,* illustrated by Anthea Sieveking. Hauppauge, NY: Barron's, 1992.

A culturally diverse group of boys & girls are photographed one at a time handling something which starts with the letter on their page.

BOARD BOOKS

Duerrstein, Richard. *In Out/Dentro Fuera; Micky is Happy/Mickey Esta Feliz; One Mickey Mouse/Un Raton Mickey.* New York: Disney, 1993.

Spanish/English versions of some simple concept books starring famous Disney cartoon characters.

Hoban, Tana. *Black on White* and *White on Black*. New York: Greenwillow, 1993.

Photographed silhouettes of familiar objects on white and black backgrounds.

MacDonald, Amy. *Let's Go* and *Let's Pretend,* illustrated by Maureen Roffey. Cambridge, MA: Candlewick, 1994.

Colorful readers for the youngest children.

Yee, Patrick. *Baby Bear, Baby Lion, Baby Monkey, Baby Penguin*. New York: Viking, 1994.

Colorful baby animal adventures which always end with Mama.

CONCEPT BOOKS

Burningham, John. *First Steps*. Cambridge, MA: Candlewick, 1994.

Burningham's classic concept books on abc, 123, opposites and colors are combined in this concept "encyclopedia" for the very young.

Butterworth, Nick & Mick Inkpen. *Jasper's Beanstalk*. New York: Bradbury, 1993.

Jasper plants, tends and digs up his beanstalk bean across the seven days of the week. Good for reading aloud or storytelling, we place it here as a good example of how the days of the week should be taught—embedded in a fun story with no other mention necessary.

Dodds, Dayle Ann. *The Color Box,* illustrated by Giles Laroche. Boston: Little, Brown, 1992.

Cut-out holes allow Alexander the monkey and the young reader to discover the next page's color.

Rossetti, Christina. *Color,* illustrated by Mary Teichman. New York: Harper, 1992.

Mary Teichman's large, bright and simple illustrations for Christina Rossetti's memorable poem make this a perfect first lesson in color.

CONTROLLED VOCABULARY BOOKS & EASY READERS

Brown, Craig. *In the Spring*. New York: Greenwillow, 1994.

In the spring all the farm animals (humans, too) have a baby or two in this simple story.

Sharratt, Nick. *Snazzy Aunties*. Cambridge, MA: Candlewick, 1994.
A boy's seven aunts visit with names to match their outfits.

COUNTING & NUMBER BOOKS

Edwards, Richard. *Ten Tall Oak Trees,* illustrated by Caroline Crossland. New York: Tambourine, 1993.

The ten tall oaks come down one-by-one over a couple hundred years until there are none. In the final double-page spread, a boy plants a seed he finds by the stumps and we see his tree begin to flourish.

Heller, Nicholas. *Ten Old Pails,* illustrated by Yossi Abolafia. New York: Greenwillow, 1994.

A boy collects 10 pails in this look at imaginative play with counting as a theme.

MacKinnon, Debbie. *How Many?,* photographs by Anthea Sieveking. New York: Dial, 1993.

Playful toddlers are illustrated in this bright and simple first counting book.

Micklethwait, Lucy. *I Spy Two Eyes: Numbers in Art.* New York: Greenwillow, 1993.

A very clever idea is made to work wonderfully well. Paintings are presented with a simple "I spy" line, e.g. I spy thirteen singers, which a young child can then find in the work shown.

Ormerod, Jan. *Joe Can Count.* New York: Mulberry, 1993.

Joe stands facing the reader and holds up his fingers to help anyone learn to count while the items he is counting are pictured in his imagination.

Merriam, Eve. *Twelve Ways to Get to Eleven,* illustrated by Bernie Karlin. New York: Scholastic, 1993.

Older preschoolers as well as those fascinated by numbers will enjoy the puzzles in this vivid picture book.

Wallace, Karen. *Why Count Sheep?: A Bedtime Book,* illustrated by Patrice Aggs. New York: Hyperion, 1993.

Folks from various occupations are pictured counting the tools of their trade, so to speak.

ENGLISH/SPANISH BOOKS

Emberley, Rebecca. *Let's Go, A Book in Two Languages/Vamos, Un Libro en Dos Lenguas.* Boston: Little, Brown, 1993.

Language learning is presented as fun in this collection of pictures with their bilingual labels.

Hill, Eric. *Spot Va al Parque.* New York: Putnam, 1992.

A Spanish version of the lift-the-flap book, Spot Goes to the Park.

Mora, Pat. *Listen to the Desert/Oye al Desierto,* illustrated by Francisco X. Mora. New York: Clarion, 1994.

Readers are asked to listen to the world around them in repeated and lyrical language—an idea well-suited to a book in two languages.

Shott, Stephen. *La Hora del la Comida.* New York: Dutton, 1992.

Eating and drinking from a baby's perspective in this Spanish only board book illustrated with colored photographs.

FOLKTALES & FAIRY TALES

Barton, Byron. *The Little Red Hen.* New York: Harper, 1993.

The classic story of the hen seeking help and finding it only when the work is finished—help in eating it. She declines that assistance!

Rounds, Glen. *Three Billy Goats Gruff.* New York: Holiday House, 1993.

Mr. Rounds' Billy Goats are formidable opponents for the troll under the bridge.

Van Laan, Nancy. *The Tiny, Tiny Boy and the Big, Big Cow,* illustrated by Marjorie Priceman. New York: Knopf, 1993.

In this folktale from Scotland a small boy finally outwits a disagreeable cow.

INFORMATIONAL BOOKS

Calmenson, Stephanie. *Rosie: A Visiting Dog's Story,* photographed by Justin Sutcliffe. New York: Clarion, 1994.

Rosie is a Tibetan terrier who is trained to bring joy into many lives as a visitor to the emotionally and physically in need.

Robbins, Ken. *Power Machines.* New York: Holt, 1993.

Hand-colored photographs of 13 awe-inspiring machines will delight the young digger/dumper types.

Wallace, Karen. *Think of a Beaver,* illustrated by Mick Manning. Cambridge, MA: Candlewick, 1993.

Beavers behave as beavers will which is fascinating to preschool children.

Wu, Norbert. *Fish Faces.* New York: Holt, 1993.

These photographs cover the range of fish faces out there, from "yikes" ugly to "oh isn't that" cute?

INFORMATIONAL BOOKS FOR CAREGIVERS, PARENTS & TEACHERS

Cole, Joanna & Stephanie Calmenson. *Pin the Tail on the Donkey and Other Party Games,* illustrated by Alan Tiegreen. New York: Morrow, 1993.

Clear illustrations and succinct advice make this a helpful guide for adults in need of new or refreshed games for their preschoolers.

Irvine, Joan. *Build it With Boxes,* illustrated by Linda Hendry. New York: Morrow, 1993.

A wonderfully useful book of ideas and directions for all sorts of boxes and containers.

Owen, Cheryl. *My Nature Craft Book.* Boston: Little, Brown, 1993.

Large, easy-to-see illustrations help the adult using this book to succeed in doing the crafts with children.

PHOTO-ILLUSTRATED BOOKS & BOOKS OF PHOTOGRAPHS

Hirschi, Ron. *A Time for Babies* (1993); *A Time for Playing* (1994); *A Time for Singing* (1994); *A Time for Sleeping* (1993), photographs by Thomas D. Mangelsen. New York: Cobblehill.

A playful concept series with animal photographs so clear and bright, young children will want to pet some of the subjects.

Miller, Margaret. *Can You Guess?* New York: Greenwillow, 1993.

A question is posed and four silly photographic answers are given before something reasonable is provided. This is the kind of humor that drives two- and three-year-olds into giggle fits.

Rotner, Shelley & Ken Kreisler. *Citybook,* photographs by Shelly Rotner. New York: Orchard, 1994.

The colorful sights of a city from a child's perspective.

PICTURE STORYBOOKS FOR THE YOUNGEST CHILDREN

Evans, Katie. *Hunky Dory Ate It,* illustrated by Janet Morgan Stoeke. New York: Dutton, 1992.

Hunky Dory will eat just about anything and love it except the medicine he needs to soothe his stomachache!

Ginsburg, Mirra. *Good Morning, Chick,* Illustrated by Byron Barton. New York: Tupelo, 1993.

A chick's first adventures in the barnyard in a small format edition of the original.

Lillie, Patricia. *Everything Has A Place,* illustrated by Nancy Tafuri. New York: Greenwillow, 1993.

A tender string of objects in their places ending with a baby on a lap and a family in a house, this is an ideal early storybook for a baby.

PICTURE STORYBOOKS HELPFUL FOR SPECIFIC SITUATIONS OR EVENTS

BABY

Koehler, Phoebe. Making Room. New York: Bradbury, 1993.

In an interesting twist on a popular theme, it is the dog who must make room for first a lady, then a cat, and finally a baby. He makes the best of each situation and always finds something good in the new arrangement.

BABYSITTER

Hines, Anna Grossnickle. *Even If I Spill My Milk?* New York: Clarion, 1994.

A boy whose parents are about to depart for a party asks lots of "testing" questions of a patient and loving mother.

BATHROOM/TOILETING

Gomi, Taro. *Everyone Poops.* New York: Kane/Miller, 1993.

The title says it all in this honest look at the most universal of animal habits.

BEDTIME

Fox, Mem. *Time for Bed,* illustrated by Jane Dyer. San Diego: Harcourt, 1993.

Young animals are put to bed by their moms as a lead-up to the young child's own bedtime.

BIRTHDAYS

Rice, Eve. *Benny Bakes a Cake.* New York: Greenwillow, 1981.

Toddler Benny loses his cake to his dog Ralph, but all ends well with the surprise delivery of a new cake.

CLEANING UP

Cummings, Pat. *Clean Your Room, Harvey Moon!* New York: Aladdin, 1994.

Harvey tries to fool his mom, but moms always learn the truth in this humorous look at a common problem.

DIVORCE/SEPARATION

Ballard, Robin. *Gracie.* New York: Greenwillow, 1993.

Gracie makes the best of traveling between parents, but finds much love in both houses.

FRIENDSHIP

Burningham, John. *The Friend.* Cambridge, MA: Candlewick, 1994.

A young boy has other friends, "of course," but Arthur is his best friend.

ILLNESS

Brown, Marc. *Arthur's Chicken Pox.* Boston: Little, Brown, 1994.

That common childhood ailment attacks beloved Arthur.

Greenfield, Eloise. *William and the Good Old Days,* illustrated by Jan Spivey Gilchrist. New York: Harper, 1993.

An older preschooler remembers the days when his grandmother was well and has hopes for good new days as well.

INDIVIDUALITY

Coplans, Peta. *Dottie*. Boston: Houghton, 1994.

A dog named Dottie persists in her wish to grow things.

Walsh, Ellen Stoll. *Hop Jump*. San Diego: Harcourt, 1993.

A frog takes up dancing and finds room for hoppers and dancers.

MOVING

Halpern, Shari. *Moving from One to Ten*. New York: Macmillan, 1993.

A counting book for a preschooler's move includes 2 angry cats and 3 worried sisters.

PARENT TRAVELING

Fowler, Susi Gregg. *I'll See You When the Moon is Full,* illustrated by Jim Fowler. New York: Greenwillow, 1994.

An adoring young boy and his sweet father come up with a way of measuring the days dad will be gone.

SCHOOL

Cooney, Nancy Evans. *Chatterbox Jamie,* illustrated by Marylin Hafner. New York: Putnam, 1993.

A young boy's first experiences at nursery school provide a comforting introduction for preschoolers.

Denslow, Sharon Phillips. *Bus Riders,* illustrated by Nancy Carpenter. New York: Four Winds, 1993.

The school bus trip provides a great deal of humor as various substitutes take over for the regular driver during his hospital stay.

Maurer, Donna. *Annie, Bea, and Chi Chi Dolores: A School Day Alphabet,* illustrated by Denys Cazet. New York: Orchard, 1993.

A busy kindergarten day provides the background for this inviting trip through the alphabet.

SECURITY BLANKETS

Henkes, Kevin. *Owen*. New York: Greenwillow, 1993.

Owen loved "Fuzzy" his yellow blanket with all his heart, but something must be done so Owen can go to school without what he will never willingly give up. His mother comes up with an excellent solution which leaves everyone happy.

SIBLINGS

Hughes, Shirley. *Bouncing*. Cambridge, MA: Candlewick, 1993.

A little girl introduces baby brother to the ways and means of bouncing.

Strub, Susanne. *My Dog, My Sister, and I.* New York: Tambourine, 1993.

A nearly six-year-old boy looks back fondly on the last two years, comparing the development of his dog Sparky and his sister Annie.

Yaccarino, Dan. *Big Brother Mike.* New York: Hyperion, 1993.

A young boy laments about not being liked by his older brother, but does remember some nice things, too, in this oddly 50's cartoon-like book.

WAKING UP

Russo, Marisabina. *Time to Wake Up!* New York: Greenwillow, 1994.

A boy and his mom get ready to start their respective days.

PICTURE STORYBOOKS WITH ANIMAL CHARACTERS

ASSORTED

Brown, Ruth. *The Picnic.* New York: Dutton, 1993.

Young listeners will be encouraged to take another's perspective in this gentle story of animals invaded by picnickers.

Chapman, Cheryl. *Pass the Fritters, Critters,* illustrated by Susan L. Roth. New York: Four Winds, 1993.

A boy can't get any of the animals to pass him their food (bear/eclair) until he remembers to say please.

Kalan, Robert. *Stop Thief!,* illustrated by Yossi Abolafia. New York: Greenwillow, 1993.

A nut travels from animal to animal until, miraculously it is accidentally returned to the original squirrel who buried it.

Wood, Jakki. *Animal Parade.* New York: Bradbury, 1993.

A long parade of all sorts of animals marches across the alphabet and from page to page.

BEARS

Arnosky, Jim. *Every Autumn Comes the Bear.* New York: Putnam, 1993.

A nicely done autumn countdown to the hibernation of an appealing bear.

Hayes, Sarah. *This is the Bear,* illustrated by Helen Craig. Cambridge, MA: Candlewick, 1993.

The bear who goes to the dump, but ends up safe in his boy's bed at story's end.

CHICKENS

Auch, Mary Jane. *Peeping Beauty.* New York: Holiday House, 1993.

Poulette wants to become a famous ballerina and does, starring as Peeping Beauty in a show where she must also foil the nasty plans of fox.

COWS

Allen, Pamela. *Belinda.* New York: Viking, 1993.

This fun-filled tale follows the adventures of a cow and her master, Tom.

Dubanevich, Arlene. *Calico Cows.* New York: Viking 1993.

The cows don't know what to do when their leader Bertha goes to the fair. Luckily, she returns at day's end to lead them home from their misadventure.

Ericsson, Jennifer A. *No Milk!,* illustrated by Ora Eitan. New York: Tambourine, 1993.

A city boy makes his first attempts at milking a cow.

DOGS

Burningham, John. *The Dog.* Cambridge, MA: Candlewick, 1994.

A dog visits and behaves mischievously, in other words, like a dog.

Hansard, Peter. *Wag Wag Wag,* illustrated by Barbara Firth. Cambridge, MA: Candlewick, 1993.

Doggy habits are fondly portrayed.

Kopper, Lisa. *Daisy Thinks She is a Baby.* New York: Knopf, 1994.

Daisy the dog "lives" the life of a human baby, but the real baby doesn't like that until Daisy becomes a mommy, and the baby loves that.

ELEPHANTS

Ford, Miela. *Little Elephant,* photographs by Tana Hoban. New York: Greenwillow, 1994.

A sweet look at a zoo dwellng baby elephant through the lens of the talented Tana Hoban.

Wahl, Jan. *Little Gray One,* illustrated by Frane Lessac. New York: Tambourine, 1993.

A day in the life of a baby elephant and his mother in the wild, with imagined conversation.

MONSTERS

Emberley, Ed. *Go Away, Big Green Monster*. Boston: Little, Brown, 1992.

A very clever cumulative tale which uses color & cut-outs to bring in and send away the big green monster.

PICTURE STORYBOOKS WITH HUMAN CHARACTERS

ADULT WITH DISABILITY AS MAIN CHARACTER

Cowen-Fletcher, Jane. *Mama Zooms*. New York: Scholastic, 1993.

A very young boy imagines all sorts of rides as he travels about in the lap of his mother who zooms everywhere in her wheelchair.

AFRICAN AMERICAN CHILD/FAMILY AS MAIN CHARACTER

Bunting, Eve. *Flower Garden*, illustrated by Kathryn Hewitt. San Diego: Harcourt, 1994.

A girl and her dad surprise mom with a window box filled with flowers for her birthday.

Falwell, Cathryn. *Feast for Ten*. New York: Clarion, 1993.

The numbers one through ten are integrated into this bright picture storybook about a mother and her children's dinner preparations.

Lotz, Karen E. *Can't Sit Still,* illustrated by Colleen Browning. New York: Dutton, 1993.

A girl celebrates the four seasons in and around her city apartment.

ASIAN AMERICAN CHILD/FAMILY AS MAIN CHARACTER

Garland, Sherry. *The Lotus Seed,* illustrated by Tatsuro Kiuchi. San Diego: Harcourt, 1993.

A seed from the imperial garden in Vietnam blossoms in the United States to remind the grandmother who picked it of the beauty of her homeland.

BABY/TODDLER AS MAIN CHARACTER

Paxton, Tom. *Where's the Baby?,* illustrated by Mark Graham. New York: Morrow, 1993.

A baby girl's day is explored in the form of a hide and seek game with the young listener.

BOY AS MAIN CHARACTER

dePaola, Tomie. *Tom.* New York: Putnam, 1993.

A grandfather teaches his grandson a trick for entertaining his school mates.

Manushkin, Fran. *Peeping and Sleeping,* illustrated by Jennifer Plecas. New York: Clarion, 1994.

On a nighttime flashlight expedition, Barry's dad introduces his son to the spring arrival of the frogs known as "peepers".

Serfozo, Mary. *Joe Joe,* illustrated by Nina S. Montezinos. New York: McElderry, 1993.

Joe Joe bang-clangs and slip-drips his way around his rural neighborhood and back home covered with mud to an understanding mom.

Shannon, George. *Climbing Kansas Mountains,* illustrated by Thomas Allen. New York: Bradbury, 1993.

A father surprises his son with a trip to climb a Kansas mountain—a grain elevator.

CHARACTERS FROM TWO OR MORE CULTURES

Patrick, Denise Lewis. *The Car Washing Street,* illustrated by John Ward. New York: Tambourine, 1993.

A sticky Saturday starts off with car washing and ends in a friendly water fight on this city street of mostly African American and Latino families.

GIRL AS MAIN CHARACTER

Curtis, Jamie Lee. *When I Was Little: A Four-Year-Old's Memoir of Her Youth,* illustrated by Laura Cornell. New York: Harper, 1993.

Four-year-olds do love looking back at their toddlerhood, all those months ago!

Noll, Sally. *Lucky Morning.* New York: Greenwillow, 1994.

Nora and her grandfather discover wild animals and some sweet time together on a vacation walk/fishing expedition in Montana.

Ransom, Candice. *The Big Green Pocketbook,* illustrated by Felicia Bond. New York: Harper, 1993.

A young girl's green pocketbook fills with treasures from the day's adventure until it is left on a bus, but heroically returned by the bus driver.

Stevenson, James. *Rolling Rose.* New York: Greenwillow, 1992.

The rolling walkers designed for babies have a mixed safety reptutation, but this rolling adventure for young Rose is imaginative and warm.

Stock, Catherine. *Where Are You Going Manyoni?* New York: Morrow, 1993.

Young Manyoni travels very far on foot until she reaches school, in this beautiful walk through the African countryside.

LATINO/HISPANIC AMERICAN CHILD/FAMILY AS MAIN CHARACTER

Gordon, Ginger. *My Two Worlds,* photographed by Martha Cooper. New York: Clarion Books, 1993.

A school-age girl is traveling to the Dominican Republic for Christmas to visit her relatives. Both of the girl's cultures are portrayed in photographs and informative text.

Reiser, Lynn. *Margaret and Margarita: Margarita Y Margaret.* New York: Greenwillow, 1993.

Two girls & their mothers meet in the park. One pair speaks only English and the other only Spanish, but the girls manage to communicate, become friends and teach the readers some new words.

POETRY & SONG BOOKS

Craig, Helen. *I See the Moon, and the Moon Sees Me . . .* New York: Harper, 1993.

A collection of nursery rhymes for all preschoolers illustrated by someone who heard plenty as a child—she thanks her mother for reading and singing these rhymes together in the dedication.

Hale, Sarah Josepha Hale. *Mary Had a Little Lamb,* photo-illustrated by Bruce McMillan. New York: Scholastic, 1990.

The classic song is beautifully photographed and although the children pictured are a bit older, preschoolers love seeing older children in picture books as well.

Loveless, Liz. *1, 2, Buckle My Shoe.* New York: Hyperion, 1993.

A picture book version of this timeless rhyme.

Rayner, Mary. *Ten Pink Piglets: Garth Pig's Wall Song. & One by One: Garth Pig's Rain Song.* New York: Dutton, 1994.

The charming Garth Pig and his family "star" in two classic songs, "Ninety-nine Bottles of Milk" and "The Ants Go Marching One by One."

READ-ALOUD FAVORITES

Archambault, John & Bill Martin, Jr. *A Beautiful Feast for a Big King Cat,* illustrated by Bruce Degen. New York: Harper, 1994.

A young mouse enjoys teasing the cat and being saved by his mom, until one tease too many allows him to escape by a whisker.

Butterworth, Nick. *The Rescue Party.* Boston: Little, Brown, 1993.

Percy the park keeper thinks he has the day off, but a rabbit rescue requires his immediate attention and the help of all his animal friends.

Johnson, Angela. *Julius,* illustrated by Dav Pilkey. New York: Orchard, 1993.

This story of a pig present from Alaska portrays a fascinating family with an amazingly clever pig.

Murphy, Jill. *A Quiet Night In.* Cambridge, MA: Candlewick, 1993.

Mrs. Large the elephant wants all the little Larges (we couldn't resist) in bed so she can celebrate her husband's birthday with a quiet night in. It gets very quiet as first Mr. and then Mrs. Large nods off leaving the kids to consume the birthday feast.

PLAY BOOKS

Cole, Joanna & Stephanie Calmenson. *Pat-A-Cake and Other Play Rhymes,* illustrated by Alan Tiegreen. New York: Morrow, 1992.

Clear directions are provided when there might be doubt, but usually it is Tiegreen's visual directions in sync with the words that make this an excellent guide to doing rhymes with babies.

Dale, Penny. *All About Alice.* Cambridge, MA: Candlewick, 1993.

Alice's day is presented in much detail in pictures & words. Questions an adult can ask the child will prompt plenty of adult/child conversation and fun.

Henderson, Kathy. *Bumpety Bump: A Lap Game Book for Babies,* illustrated by Carol Thompson. Cambridge, MA: Candlewick, 1994.

A baby is bounced and tumbled about in this loving look at playing with a baby.

Offen, Hilda. *A Fox Got My Socks.* New York: Dutton, 1993.

A baby leads the reader through some "whole body" play to accompany the text of this simple list of animals and the clothing items they've "got"

Stott, Dorothy. *Kitty and Me.* New York: Dutton, 1993.

A lift-and-look flap book with kitty having most of the adventures.

STORYBOOKS ESPECIALLY SUITABLE FOR STORYTELLING

USING FELTBOARD & FELT PIECES

Brisson, Pat. *Benny's Pennies,* illustrated by Bob Barner. New York: Doubleday, 1993.

Barner's torn paper illustrations suggest one method of creating scenery in this
cumulative tale of a boy who trades for something for everyone.

Brown, Margaret Wise. *The Quiet Noisy Book* (other titles include *The Quiet
Book, The Seashore Noisy Book, The Summer Noisy Book*), illustrated
by Leonard Weisgard. New York: Harper, 1950.

Weisgard's bold & geometrically fascinating illustrations are fun for small numbers, but hard to see in a large group, allowing Brown's words an alternate
path to the ears of her listeners.

USING PROPS

Carlstrom, Nancy White. *Rise and Shine!,* illustrated by Dominic Catalano.
New York: Harper, 1993.

Simple rhymes make this story of a little girl greeting the animals on her farm
suited for toddlers who would love to see three-dimensional animals receive
that greeting.

APPENDIX B
BOOKS ABOUT SELECTING, USING & ENJOYING CHILDREN'S LITERATURE

Check the resource & reference sections at the end of each chapter for books on the specific topics covered in that chapter.

DeSalvo, Nancy N. *Beginning with Books: Library Programming for Infants, Toddlers and Preschoolers.* Hamden, CT: Shoe String Press, 1993.

Donavin, Denise Perry. *Best of the Best for Children.* New York: Random House & The American Library Association, 1992.

Greene, Ellin. *Books, Babies and Libraries: Serving Infants, Toddlers, Their Parents & Caregivers.* Chicago: American Library Association, 1991.

Hearne, Betsy. *Choosing Books for Children: A Commonsense Guide.* New York: Delacorte, 1990.

McGovern, Edythe M. & Helen D. Muller. *They're Never Too Young for Books: A Guide to Children's Books For Ages 1 to 8.* Buffalo: Prometheus Books, 1994.

Rudman, Masha K. & Anna Pearce. *For Love of Reading: A Parent's Guide to Encouraging Young Readers and Writers from Infancy Through Age Five.* Mount Vernon, NY: Consumers Union, 1988.

APPENDIX C
MAGAZINES FOR CHILDREN

Ladybug, The Magazine for Young Children
315 Fifth Street, Box 300, Peru, Il 61354
Subscription Address: P.O. Box 58342, Boulder, CO 80322
(815) 223-1500

This monthly, preschool version of the famous Cricket Magazine is the finest children's literature magazine for young children on the market.

Sesame Street Magazine
1 Lincoln Plaza, New York, NY 10023
Subscription Address: P.O. Box 55518, Boulder, CO 80322
(800) 678-0613

A fine way to connect the Sesame Street fan to the printed word is this 10 issue a year television-based magazine.

Your Big Backyard
1400 16th Street, NW, Washington, DC 20036
(202) 797-6800
Subscription Address: 8925 Leesburg Pike, Vienna, VA 22189
(800) 432-6564

Learning is bright, colorful & fun in this publication of the National Wildlife Federation.

APPENDIX D
MAGAZINES ABOUT CHILDREN'S LITERATURE AND CHILDREN

Day Care and Early Education
Human Sciences Press, Inc.
233 Spring Street
New York, NY 10013
(212) 620-8000
– quarterly
– information for early childhood
    educators & day care
    administrators

Booklist
American Library Association
50 East Huron Street
Chicago, IL 60611
(800) 545-2433
– published twice monthly except July
    and August where it is monthly
– children's book reviews

*Bulletin of the Center for Children's
  Books*
University of Illinois Press
54 East Gregory Drive
Champaign, IL 61820
(217) 333-0950
– published monthly except August
– children's book reviews

*The Horn Book Guide to
  Children's and Young Adult
  Books*
11 Beacon Street, Suite 1000
Boston, MA 02108
(800) 325-1170
– published twice annually
– briefly reviews all children's
    books published in the United
    States in previous six months

Horn Book Magazine
11 Beacon Street, Suite 1000
Boston, MA 02108
(617) 227-1555
– published bimonthly
– children's book reviews

Young Children
National Association for the
  Education of Young Children
1834 Connecticut Avenue, NW
Washington DC 20009
(202) 232-8777
– published bimonthly
– information for early childhood
    educators & administrators

APPENDIX E
SELECTED
PROFESSIONAL
ORGANIZATIONS
SERVING THE NEEDS
OF CHILDREN

Children's Defense Fund
25 E Street, NW
Washington, DC 20001
(202) 628-8787

Council for Exceptional Children
1920 Association Drive
Reston, VA 22091
(703) 620-3660

Head Start
P.O. Box 1182
Washington, DC 20013
(202) 205-8572

National Association for the Education of Young Children
1509 16th Street, NW
Washington, DC 20036-1426
(800) 424-2460

APPENDIX F SELECTED PROFESSIONAL ORGANIZATIONS THAT PROMOTE CHILDREN'S LITERATURE

Association for Library Service
    to Children
a division of the American Library
    Association
50 East Huron Street
Chicago, IL 60611
(800) 545-2433 ext. 2163

Association of Booksellers
    for Children
4412 Chowen South #303
Minneapolis, MN 55410
(800) 421-1665

Children's Book Council
568 Broadway, Suite 404
New York, NY 10012
(212) 966-1990

National Association for the
    Preservation and Perpetuation
    of Storytelling
P.O. Box 309
Jonesborough, TN 37659
(615) 753-2171

International Reading Association
800 Barksdale Road
PO Box 8139
Newark, DE 19714-8139
(302) 731-1600

Society of Children's Book Writers
    & Illustrators
22736 Van Owen Street, Suite 106
West Hills, CA 91307
(818) 888-8760

Teachers as Readers Project
Association of American Publishers
71 5th Avenue
New York, NY 10003
(212) 255-0200

United States Board on Books
    for Young People, Inc.,
    Secretariat
(the United States Section of
    the International Board on
    Books for Young People)
c/o International Reading
    Association
800 Barksdale Road
PO Box 8139
Newark, DE 19714-8139
(302) 731-1600, ext. 274

INDEX

Steven Herb is Education Librarian and Collection Development Specialist for Children's Literature at the Pennsylvania State University and the former Coordinator of Children's Services for the Dauphin County Library System in Harrisburg, Pennsylvania.

Sara Willoughby-Herb is Professor of Early Childhood Education and Nursery Teacher in the Laboratory School at Shippensburg University of Pennsylvania.